Dec 3

To: Atula Govinda Dasa

Sweet Serenity

My first book!

Haribol,

Steven

December 30, 2023

To: Atula Govinda Dasa,

My first book!

Haribol,

Steven

SWEET SERENITY

A POETIC SPIRITUAL JOURNEY

STEVEN LEONARD SCHWARTZ

Steven Leonard Schwartz

IMAGO
PRESS
TUCSON ARIZONA

Published in the United States of America by:

Imago Press
3710 East Edison
Tucson AZ 85716

Library of Congress Control Number: 2014955766

Book Design by Leila Joiner

ISBN 978-1-935437-91-8
ISBN 1-935437-91-7

Printed in the United States of America on Acid-Free Paper

FORWARD
by Friends of George Harrison

Author of *Here Comes the Sun*, Joshua Greene

You can't get enough of Schwartz
Once you've tasted his writing
You'll need more than quarts—
He's an ocean of delighting.

Author of *By His Example* and *Love, Medicine and Music*, Gurudas took shelter of Srila Prabhupada, as his spiritual master in 1967. After reading Schwartz's poem, "The Guru Man," written for him, he responded with a poem in return (12/02/12).

Steven Steven you da man
Your heart is full
You ain't no sham

Thank you friend, Steven
Your poetry stops all grieving
Your appreciation encourages me
Flower to flower like a bee

THANK YOU

Dr. Luke S. Albert, Sunny Arfa, Aaron Briese, Kent Brown, VeronicaCastro, Scot Coogan, Alice Cooper, Larry Cornwall and Alice In Cooperland, Dustin Cox, dandavats.com, Mahatma Das, Manvantar Das, Sunanda Das, Sura Das, Kirtan Yajna Das, Bhima Dasa,Caturbava Dasa, Nirantara Dasa Acbsp, Titiksava Karunika Dasa,Paloma Devi, Sandamini Devi Dasi, Wim de Lang, Gary England,FOR GEORGE, Duane and Genie Forkner, Richard Freede, Lynette Brown Fromong, Kendall Gillens, Govinda's of Tucson & ISKCON of Arizona at Tucson, Joshua Greene, David Guhin, Gurudas, Heather Harris, Sharon Harris, Nimai Hemphill, Frank Hoopes, Leila Joiner and Imago Press, Rhonda Jordan, Simrit Kaur Khalsa, Snatam Kaur Khalsa, krishna.com, Krishna Cove - Tucson, Krishna Lounge - Las Vegas, Kevin Leonard, Aaron Lieberman, Lilly and Friends, ISKCONWestern World Headquarters Los Angeles and Svavasa Dasa, AndreMcCarroll, Nancy MacMillan, Daniel Maloney, Larry Manning, Randy Nauert, Rob Nieuwveld, Tim O'Brien, Gabriel Odisho, WynneParis, Madana Peat and Sundarananda Das of ISKCON Honolulu, Chris Piva, Luis Reyes and Sin City KISS, BensonAlexander Riseman, Mike Salisbury, Josh Scherer, Bagel and LoxieSchwartz, Barry Schwartz, Gerald Schwartz, Joanne Schwartz,Simmie K. Schwartz, Susan Schwartz, Tere Scott, Murray Silver, GuruGanesha Singh and The GuruGanesha Band, JackieSlater-Kanaley, Traci Smith, Steffanie Stapleton, Bryan Thomas, JadeUno, Yogi Girl Yogi Guy, Diane Vanderpool-Haag, Jivananda DasaVanacari, and WAH!

Special thanks to my wife, Simmie K. Schwartz, in assisting 24/7 with final editing of *Sweet Serenity.*

PREFACE

The seeds for *Sweet Serenity* were planted on a cool September morning way back in 1974 when WBCN, Boston's FM rock radio station, announced ex-Beatle George Harrison would be performing at Boston Garden in December.

I waited all night long on November 3rd for the Garden box office to open the next morning at 10:00 AM. You couldn't sleep in those old, rickety, wooden Boston Garden seats, but you dozed now and then. Surrounded by thousands desiring to be part of rock and roll history seeing George Harrison on tour, we were Hari-Fans ready for our first George-Fest. That's how it began, "All Those Years Ago."

George meant more to me now than ever as his spirituality and relationship to a higher being solidified my spiritual journey. A day didn't pass without my thinking of George or writing something in my journal that happened to me based on his song lyrics. Just ask my college friend, Larry Manning. After discussing a George tune, we would end the conversation with Frank Zappa's legendary title, "It Can't Happen Here," like a skit from Saturday Night Live. My "All Things Must Pass" album was so worn out by continuous playing on an old stylus that it gave new meaning to "Snap, Crackle, & Pop," the Rice Krispies cereal.

Sweet Serenity is dedicated to the life of George Harrison. I created poetry from photographs of George, thinking what he would say to me based upon the images. It was important to show the loving relationship George had with Krishna and his beautiful gardens at his Friar Park home.

The book was completed over a three-year period and contains nine chapters. You are invited to read every section, as there is something for everyone to enjoy.

I am sure *Sweet Serenity* will be a very pleasurable experience for you. Readers can embark on their own spiritual journey, so "The Long and Winding Road" of life won't be so treacherous anymore. George's friend, Gurudas, loves my poetry! It is his opinion George would love it, too!

Steven Leonard Schwartz
Tucson, Arizona
April 3, 2014

AUTHOR'S STATEMENT

Steven Leonard Schwartz began writing poetry three years ago on his brother's veranda overlooking the Pacific Ocean. He closed his eyes, dreamed, and wrote poetic themes listening to waves of devotion. Influenced by George Harrison, Krishna, nature and spirituality, *Sweet Serenity* will lift you higher in your desire to cope with life's reality. Steven and his wife, Simmie, live with their parakeets, Bagel and Loxie, in Henderson, Nevada.

NOTES ON PHOTOGRAPHS

Photographs provided by Gurudas for *Sweet Serenity* are the property of Gurudas. He was the photographer in many and procured other photographs from various sources back in the day. Images were also photographed for him. Gurudas served Krishna for the benefit of *Sweet Serenity.* I asked Gurudas why was he providing these photographs for *Sweet Serenity.* He replied, "Sometimes Krishna surprises on the upside."

Photographs provided by Mike Salisbury for *Sweet Serenity* are the property of Mike Salisbury, and are accompanied by his copyright. Mike photographed George for the cover photo of Harrison's eighth album, entitled "George Harrison."

Photographs provided by Murray Silver for *Sweet Serenity* are the property of Murray Silver, and are accompanied by his copyright. Murray photographed George Harrison in Atlanta, Georgia for George's Dark Horse Tour of North America in 1974. The two (2) Murray Silver images of George Harrison are unpublished photographs. They are being published for the first time in *Sweet Serenity.*

Steven Leonard Schwartz

Tucson Botanical Gardens

The administration of Tucson Botanical Gardens, Tucson, Arizona authorized Steven Leonard Schwartz to photograph plants and flowers for publication in his poetry book, *Sweet Serenity*.

Peacock Mandala Shawl

Paul Heussentenstamm is the artist who created the Peacock Mandala Shawl worn by Steven Leonard Schwartz in *Sweet Serenity*. The shawl can be seen in the following locations:

Chapter 3

A Little Bit of Krishna

Chapter 5

Pure Ecstasy

The Back Cover of the Book

An 11-inch square portrait of the Peacock Mandala Shawl & the Peacock Shawl can be purchased at: www.circlesoflightimports.com

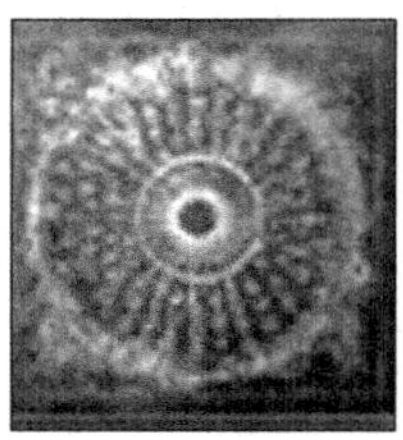

TABLE OF CONTENTS

DEDICATION to George Harrison

Photograph courtesy of Gurudas

Hari George

It all began with Hari George
"All Those Years Ago"
He survived through all the Beatles years
Then told them where to go

George taught the world to chant and pray
In numbers innumerable to score
He opened his heart from "Behind That Locked Door"
His only desire was to love God more

CHAPTER I
George Harrison & Friends

Chapter 1 Photograph Credits

Photographs Are the Property of Gurudas
Unless Otherwise Noted

A Conversation with John

Your mind can't "Imagine" what I have to say
It's not as simple as "Lay Lady Lay" but more like "Another Day"
If it's about the band, George, make it crystal clear and without haste
All right, John, it's time Paul drop his attitude and give up the smirk on his face

I'm the number one Beatle writing his best stuff
My album play isn't anywhere near quite enough
You two have been on top gathering dust way too long
My tunes deserve an opportunity to be the band's number one songs

Nobody's music on this album compares to mine
"Here Comes The Sun" and "Something" were written for the divine
Neither you nor Paul nor Ringo have much of anything on the album
All that's there, in my opinion, is baby food and pablum

OK George, you've made a great point
Let's go somewhere and light up this joint
It's all right, John, when I'm with Krishna, I'm never alone
If that rocker guy left Cat's Cradle, maybe it's time for me to go home

George said, Being with Krishna, I am always "Home Sweet Home"
My new friend Steven just wrote this incredible poem
He pulled his "Instant Karma" together "Being for the Benefit of Mr. Kite"
Great poem, said John, Yes, Steven surely has a knack when he writes

A My Sweet Lord New Year

There will be many days just like this
Overflowing with love and filled with Krishna bliss
Lord Krishna leads us as we give praise and reminisce
Caturbhava Dasa accompanying me extols "It just doesn't get any better than this"

A kirtan in the streets of London all night long with "My Sweet Lord"
Jivananda Dasa Vanacari reads purports from the one book we can all afford
Sandamini Devi Dasi always smiling, all the way from Tucson, Arizona
Chants Hare Krishna and says, My Lord, it's my pleasure to know Ya

Hari George and Gurudas are in the main car at Prabhupada's aide
Drinking Yamuna's concoction nectar, it's her spiritual Kool-Aide
The thousands of devotees following Prabhupada are smiling along the way
Today is like "Yesterday" as every day is a Hare Krishna Holy Holiday

Tonight in Bhaktivedanta Manor and in every Krishna Temple at midnight
All around the world when the old year is wound up real real tight
George approaches the microphone as he bangs on Buddha's gong
The new year is rung in, so Hari's Son sings "Ding Dong Ding Dong"

A Portrait in Time

"A Portrait in Time" of our time spent together
That's most important, it don't matter the weather

The love we share everyday with each other
Our depth of field I just pressed the shutter

A bond connects us wherever we are
Krishna sees to it He's my shining star

The Hollies sang, "He Ain't Heavy He's My Brother"
I loved them both, Tom and Dickie, The Brothers Smothers

Until next time, it's "All Right Now"
Protect the ruminant our friend the cow

Lord Krishna is our life's inspector
Serve Krishna well His love will protect you

At Friar Park Henley (with Gurudas and Mukunda)

At Friar Park Henley, the magic starts when the sky gets dark
George Harrison tunes the instruments and then the music sparks
Playing the ukulele and banjo till the sun rises up, George is the master entertainer
Happy living with the Lord day after day, he's grateful Krishna is His permanent sustainer

The footsteps of Sir Frankie Crisp echo all over the place
George's Gothic Revival provides shelter from the material race
Never seen without his pitchfork, happy as a newborn babe delivered "In the Still of the Night"
Pruning, planting, watering and chanting, Lord Krishna tells George, "Don't Think Twice It's All Right"

Be Like This

I wish every day would be like this
Overflowing with joy and filled with bliss
The horizon in the distance has been sun-kissed
The morning dew has spread its mist

Lord, You remove the darkness from my view
By rising the sun with its golden hue
The glow You provide shines on me through You
I show my appreciation in loving devotion to You

Standing in a grassy knoll scattered among the evergreens
One of the most beautiful days in a while we've seen
I must work harder, Lord, to feel You deep inside
You're within me and all about me, You are my "Ironside"

"What Is Life," Oh Lord, what is it really about
It's all about friends, reminiscing, and Krishna no doubt
This afternoon Mukunda, Gurudas, and Derek are accompanying me
Please handle me carefully, I am happy and carefree

Gurudas is smiling and pointing due west towards the afternoon sun
My posse said, You arrived on the property about quarter to one
Krishna, Your sweet nectar makes me feel really kind of mellow
That's because I'm a "Dark Horse" kind of fellow

Behind the Pitchfork

He's the doctor of plants
Knows his xylem and phloem
Britain's master of horticulture
George knows how to show 'em

Gardening's my life
I love watching plants grow
They don't talk back to me
Like Paul McCartney, you know

This is my garden after all
I love nurturing Mother Earth
It's what I really care about
Lord Krishna and rebirth

Compost under my fingernails
Get down and dirty, you see
No more getting derailed from
A tune by Lennon-McCartney

Move a hill over here
Run the river over there
From "Behind the Pitchfork"
You see my eyes stare

My love and compassion for Krishna
A deep rooted passion in fashion
Krishna keeps my life on a spiritual mission
What a blessing always blissing

The world don't know
What it's really missing
Ears that won't listen
A mind that keeps dissin'

Will the inhabitants of our planet
Ever stop and smell the roses
If they're not trying to keep up
Materially, with the Jones's

Keep playing my records and listening to the music
Remember the lyrics, their meaning still grooves it
Because of You, all things must never pass
Love to Gurudas, a blast from my past

Come Back Home

I see You Krishna in the rear view mirror
As Your shadow follows me, I quiver in a shiver
Freedom of mobility in the world's open space
Is rapidly being diminished as I remain displaced

Contemplating my complex life is sometimes complicated
I'm wrestling with the masked maya who's ruthless and hated
I can't cope, Krishna, please make it go away
Show me how to overcome so You can raise my arm in victory

The strength to resist is not automatic
I can't find Your channel if there's too much static
The force of previous bad habits is still instilled
Not always standing with You I'm "The Fool on the Hill"

You know all my lies and see through every disguise
Today is the day I become intoxicated with nectar and permanently rise
Krishna, You know I'm good enough to "Come Back Home" where I belong
They're waiting for me now, we're singing the "Hare Krishna Maha Mantra" song

For Bob, George, and Jim

Live in the moment every step of the way
Live for right now 'cause that's what I say
Connect yourself to the rebirth of our Mother Earth
There's gonna be a long line, so hurry up and be the first

Don't you see the world has this desperate thirst
Whoever's in first place is gonna eventually be worse
When the bottom obtains wisdom they will later be first
As our leaders get too cocky, get ready to call the hearse

Burn through the flames it's your eternal desire
Nourish your soul with music from Bob and George's inspire
May they always take you further to go higher and higher
Hey Jim, open your door, go ahead and "Light My Fire"

George Harrison's Mike Salisbury

No, they didn't name Salisbury Beach after him in Essex County
Boating, fishing, and picnicking are essential to its summer bounty
North of Crane Beach in Ipswich, Salisbury is loved for its simplicity and appeal
The quaint New England town just north of Boston is absolutely ideal

"Stand By Me" within the flora and fauna of Friar Park's finest
Are Mike Salisbury and George Harrison – the photographic artist and the guitarist
On the George Harrison album, Mike glorified his friend gently touching the camera's shutter
"If You Believe" the clouds will "Blow Away," there's no need to seek out cover

GEORGE TOWN

It's been a long long time
Since you turned me on
The feelin's still there
The flame burns strong

The love you show for Krishna
It's everywhere I hear your sound
That Harrison beat leaves me mellow and sweet
Gonna meditate in GEORGE TOWN

It takes so long to know you're there
Don't wanna see you frown
Your funky sound lifts me high off the ground
Gonna levitate in GEORGE TOWN

The mantra you created
For everyone to realize
Echoes through my cranium
To the sockets of my eyes

It's so sweet and filled with joy
A present for the Lord
Standing at Your lotus feet
Everybody come aboard

Wanna see You
Wanna know You
Wanna be with You
That's true

Wanna show You
Everlasting peace
The world will go with You

Hare Krishna George

The riffs and chords from his guitar strings
Become alive when the old Gretsch sings
George triggers the love that Krishna brings
Bhaktivedanta smiles when his message rings

His music creates a transcendental state
Opens my mind to Krishna, A.C.'s running mate
Heartfelt lyrics open up Lord Krishna's gate
That's the spiritual path I want to take

George's love still lives, yes I can tell
I'm living proof his spirit is well
Received a call from Miss O'Dell
With a Cheshire smile, I see Bhaktivedanta kvell

His desire for Krishna keeps shining through
George's light illuminates my consciousness, it's true
Keep chanting with Krishna as every day begins anew
Bhaktivedanta's dream lives on within me and within you

Just Certified Gold

George heard the news on the 14th day
The year 1970 in the month of December
You've done the work Prabhupada did say
Krishna said be humble, this you should remember

My devotee George, your "My Sweet Lord" single was just certified gold
When you chant the Lord's Holy Name it is very special to behold
It makes me smile knowing you're chanting Krishna in your music recording
The world is following you and to me it is very rewarding

Mike Salisbury
VENICE
legendary branding
and writing/photography/smart remarks
mikesalisbury.net

Krishna's Way

Hey Jack, I'm a spiritual beanstalk, just looking for a better view
Leaning on the cinder blocks, Krishna, my apical meristem yearns for You
The seed Harry and Louise planted has borne fruit, such a sweet nectar
Serving You with everlasting love, My Lord, I can never fill Your spectre

Every moment with You is special, it's not just "Another Day"
You've given me Your love to breathe and a pathway to walk Your way
I've left the door open, Krishna, so You can enter on Your own accord
The world must always remember that You are "My Sweet Lord"

Life Stands Still

It's abomination the domination life has over us
We oxidize our lives away to nothing then galvanize our soul to rust
We seek not the truth for my brother's weight is too heavy as a matter of trust
So forgone are we, there's no liberty, our thoughts are stuck in the gutter of lust

When the spark in your heart says go make the change
Do anything, go anywhere, rather than be deranged
Sometimes you gotta take a break from your "Home on the Range"
When you think you're crazy, George Harrison's "Cosmic Empire" don't seem so strange

For a time, Patty, we "Let It Be" until Krishna just changed my style
"Life Stands Still" but we found that groove for a little while
It's all right, Patty, you felt the tapper from my ole friend, Clapper
My life changed really for the better 'cause he was so dapper

Dhani and Olivia consume my life, a handsome son and a beautiful wife
My days at Friar Park provide an avenue for me to live with no grief
Hey Beethoven, if you roll over this way, go ahead and make my day
Switch off the light, say goodnight, and send Tchaikovsky on his way

My Eyes Stare

I look to the left and then to the right
Lord Krishna is there to my delight
You remove the darkness from my sight
So my eyes can focus on Your rays of light

Krishna, whenever I glance in Your direction
I find myself in deep introspection
Am I worthy of Your love and affection
All I really want to see is Your reflection

I put on my goggles and pull on the straps
Zeroing in on You Krishna is totally where I'm at
Resembling Rocket J. Squirrel I race to You "In My Life"
Laughing like Bullwinkle in life's material cartoon
Gurudas eliminates my strife daily at high noon

My Krishna consciousness I am well aware
I see You Lord, "Here, There, and Everywhere"
To catch a glimpse of You by "My Eyes Stare"
I love You, Lord, with my last breath of air

"My Sweet Lord," shelter me in Your rose garden
May I serve You with a soft heart that never hardens
I loved You immensely throughout the facade of stardom
Especially at The Concert for Bangladesh in Madison Square Garden

My Favorite Ex-Beatle

The late bloomer matures and finally comes of age
Down the stretch they come, this "Dark Horse" is the rage
Stuck behind the entry, favorites to win, John and Paul
He's the one who said, I'd like to introduce a friend of us all

He hid behind the shadows lurking next to a full moon
Little did anyone know he was about to break out of his cocoon
He won the race passing them all, victorious in late June
No winners' circle photograph, his gratification is his next tune

The name of my jockey is Krishna, he announced humbly out loud
The clouds have a silver lining when Krishna's name is chanted with the sound
I care for Him with loving devotion, he is proud to say aloud
"Something" is said how His Jockey grooves, rumbles throughout the endearing crowd

My Love Grows

Krishna is my number one fan
He watches over me wherever I stand
Krishna takes care of my cares and woes
He loves me whenever my heart glows

Krishna absorbs the sins for us
In a way He's like Jesus Christ
When having prasadam at Bhaktivedanta Manor
Krishna says I'll have another bite

Krishna's feel is absolutely ideal
Krishna returns to me His love so real
He surrounds me with His aura from head to toe
Krishna loves it when my feelings show

Krishna is the One who gives me peace
And nobody really knows but me
I love it when I feel that material world release
No longer just me, now it's Krishna We

Never Outshine the Truth

Remember me for what I stand for
Not the times I walked out the revolving door
Give the other three a kick on the rump a little bit more
Because they made me sore, then like an eagle, I soared

I'll take my share of the fab four blame
But it was the other guys who drove me insane
When Yoko Ono came in – it was the end of the game
Not much left behind, but plenty of pain

My fame will "Never Outshine the Truth"
Never wanted it as a youngster "Forever Young" in my youth
Louise and Harry taught me morals while watching Hazel Booth
But it was Gurudas who led me to Krishna on the Apple roof

May the truth ring out loud and clear within my music and lyrics
May it stand the test of time so everyone can hear it
"My Sweet Lord," Dear Krishna, always be my spirit
May "Govinda" clear my mind of all the darkness that's near it

Chant Hare Krishna, Hare Krishna
May the Lord always be with you
Sing "Om Namah Shivaya," Let Krishna take you higher
Say goodbye to maya (hasta la vista and sayonara)

Never Stopped Thinking (About You)

You led me outta here
To a place much more clear
A destination a lot sweeter
Within the pages of my *Bhagavad-Gita*

Because of Your sacred ties
I've become Krishnatized
Singing about the Lord no matter the tide
High or low, Krishna's always by my side

My weary eyes still weep
Hearing that Harrison beat
Your riffs and chords so sleek
Possess Krishna's rhythm and mystique

You said, "All Things Must Pass"
But I knew our love would last
Your message keeps Krishna in view
Your music, George, has the world loving you

The sun shines bright on your horizon today
Let's go to Bhaktivedanta Manor to chant and pray
Prabhupada still has plenty to say
Take the next exit to The Hare Krishna Highway

Krishna is pulling on your coattails
He's the wind behind your spiritual sails
His love is herculean it never derails
Regardless of a hurricane, tornado or hail

Because of Your reality
My lungs breathe Krishnality
My heart beats Krishna vitality
Krishna loves my attitude and personality

Give me a smile on the way to Mandalay
Just a glimpse of You and it will be OK
I'll read you a poem, George, and we will be on our way
My orange glow sunrise sets the stage for another day

You said, "All Things Must Pass"
But I knew our love would last
Your message keeps Krishna in view
Your music, George, keeps the world loving you

Not So Instant Karma

Your Karma was not so instant when Yoko Ono became involved
Anything we were doing became unglued as the puzzle turned unsolved
You threw a monkey wrench into the arena when "All You Need Is Love" wasn't
"Lovely Rita"
Yoko and Paul together were enough to cause us seven years that were leaner
Maybe it was good you sped things up, I watched everything happen so much "Faster"
My freedom delivered by a penguin, igloo direct, via Fairbanks, Alaska

On the Road with Hari

His friend cried out
These people need help
Can you reach out and lend a hand
On August first, 1971
George assembled an all-star band

The Concert for Bangladesh was performed
In New York's Madison Square Garden
George raised a quarter of a million dollars
For refugees who were starvin'

Leon, Ringo, Eric and Billy
Were rockin', rappin', and chillin'
We all remember when he walked on stage
The legendary Bob Dylan

George toured the states in '74
Lord Krishna paved his course
His new hit single just released
The tune was called "Dark Horse"
Raspy throat – voice gone at the source
He dubbed the song, "hoarse horse"

Thirty dates in November and December
Mixed opinions from the media and press
Reviews George didn't care to read
They only made him depressed

He went back into his cave
For a couple of decades
Until a friend said, Let's go to Japan
George fluttered about Osaka and Tokyo like a merry "Peter Pan"

Having the time of his life with pal, Eric Clapton
Audiences cheered as their hands were clappin'
"Psycho guitar" was slappin', strappin', and rappin'
George bid an arigato adieu, the concert was a happenin'

One More Time

"One More Time," one more chord
One more verse of "My Sweet Lord"
To hear your voice once again
Echo from the rafters of old Boston Garden

Give me a chance to rhyme
With Krishna, Your divine
"I'd Have You Anytime"
They say, "He's So Fine"

The leaves are falling from the trees
As Bob Dylan is blowing through the breeze
Let me catch a glimpse of the "Wilbury Twist"
Through a Friar Park fog and the morning mist
"Here Comes the Sun" the day is sun kissed

To see you perform once again
Without any of your first band jive
Your second band kept you so alive
The Wilbury beat was quite a surprise

So much you have given
From the days you've liven
Your music has so much value
My pleasure to behold and to have you

Our Jukebox to Heaven

I'm a "Travelin' Man" Oh Lord, my 45's are spinning
Because I love You, Krishna, I'm always winning
My "Ding Dong Ding Dong" bells ring on with the year's end setting sun
Played many a "Garden Party" like my friend, Rick Nelson

We both got booed with our 70's styles and changing lives
You do what you can to survive, Hari Bol, reach higher and strive
You adapt and adjust, just don't lie there and gather dust
"Hitchin' a Ride" to be "Close to You," thumbs up for Krishna or bust

"Give Peace A Chance" Oh Lord, a place to begin, our life's record You spin
Our next tune is in queue, You give Ricky and me a much clearer view
No more "Lonesome Town" 'cause Lord, You're always around
Your record's playing there's no delaying – Your love's spinning round with the sound

Our parents so caring and loving, victorious warriors
Always behind us, supportive rebels in our cause
The Harrison's, The Nelson's, Harry & Louise, Ozzie & Harriet
Stepping up those mahogany steps in Your beloved chariot
They'll "Never Be Anyone Else But You" be our "True Love"- please—

Peace

I need to sit in some peace today with Pattie and bandmate John
Nice to chill out sometimes 'cause the internal pressure is always on
It's only the beginning with Krishna, it's only just the start
Gurudas says Krishna and our devotee friends will never be apart

Krishna is so important for me to keep on truckin' on
I need Him "In My Life" to remind me I belong
My fear of darkness tells me there's no longer a need to beware
Krishna always beats in my heart, no worries, no need to fear

The Hare Krishna Helicopter

Frail and meek like a withering flower
"Blowin' in the Wind" fading by the hour
Krishna, give me the strength to sustain any miscomfort or pain
Don't turn me into a pillar of salt, just let me remain

Going to pay my dues if I have my druthers
My love for You is not like all the others
I have to feel Your presence from my head down to my toes
Krishna, it's too soon for me to change my clothes

I'm sometimes too far away to get to You
More devoted service and chanting I know is the cue
I'm too weak and disheveled in this material soap opera
Fly me to You Lord in the Hare Krishna Helicopter

My emotions in the human condition just make me frown
It's hard to smile when I've got "The Tears of a Clown"
Krishna, please let me follow in Your tailwind's direction
What text and verse is this week's purport selection

© MURRAY SILVER

The Only One – One of a Kind

I'm striving for Vrindavan, it's for you, Krishna, my heart yearns
Standing alone in the coliseum of life, this devotee has a lot to learn
When we're together, Oh Krishna, it's very easy to be victorious
Everything You do, "My Sweet Lord," is so remarkable and glorious

I bask in the aura of Your sparkling effervescence
Illuminated by the shadow of Your essence
I take shelter under Your lotus feet
You're "Still the One" who makes my heart beat

Krishna, I flourish daily by performing Your service
You strengthen my soul and eliminate my nervous
The feelings I feel are ideal and are absolutely real
You bring me joy and You've got Prabhupada's zeal

The smile on Your face can never be erased
You're the antidote for the material world and the human race
I don't need to believe in anyone else
Lord Krishna, You are top shelf and are my real wealth

GEORGE HARRIS

While My George Divinely Smiles

Krishna, Your rays of love are muted by passing clouds of material attachment
My heart beats Hare Krishna as my lungs breathe maya harassment
George Harrison's guitar is always crying
When I'm not with You, Lord, I'm Krishna maya-ing

Krishna, "Brainwash" me so I can really understand
How sweet it is, when You take hold of my hand
Don't You hear George Harrison sighing
When I'm not with You, Lord, I'm Krishna dying

Krishna, the world speaks rudely to me, says it's only a joke
Corporate monoliths of steel and concrete produce despair and a lack of hope
George Harrison's guitar is barely creeping
When I'm not with You, Lord, I'm Krishna sleeping

Krishna, I'm longing and yearning as life's clock is ticking and turning
The devil looks up and sees the place burning
George Harrison's guitar is in need of repair
When I'm not with You, Lord, I'm Krishna impaired

Krishna, everybody knows the world's emperors have new clothes
They can't fathom beyond the boundary of where their kingdom goes
George Harrison's love for Krishna is never disguised
When I'm not with You, Lord, I'm Krishna compromised

Outside my door it's all reeling and riling
Everyone's a zombie their brains are frying
Like politicians today deceiving and beguiling
Clean up this mess before I even stop trying

Titiksava Karunika Dasa's guitar keeps George Harrison dreaming
The black Gretsch has stopped crying and is now Krishna healing
Sitting here with George our tea is English Twining
George Harrison's guitar is now divinely smiling

WIM DO-LANG DO-LANG

My pal Wim, it ain't no whim
It's no wonder why I'm so fond of him
From a small town not too far from Amsterdam
By George, Wim is Holland's number one Harrison fan

Wim loves George as much or more than me
He's my European George Harrison Connnection, you see
Wim's got every magazine, 45 and 33 LP
Has a Cadence label, Phil and Don, The Everly Brothers, "Let It Be Me"

Gurudas brought Krishna to George with Mukunda and Shyamasundar
Getting better over the years, George has always been my shining star
Loves Lord Krishna and avoids hanging out in the prime time
Because "Honey Don't" discotheque don't mix with "The Divine"

Hari Son invited and welcomed us to chant, "My Sweet Lord"
"After All These Years" George has given us so many lovely riffs and chords
Warning us to "Beware of Darkness" and "Think for Yourself"
"One Fine Day," George, we will realize Krishna is "The Only Wealth"

For His Blue

Just as sweet with his own Harrison beat
Dhani has me dancing up out of my seat
The kid has a voice that can't be forged
A little different from his ole man, "Papa George"

Son of George and Olivia it has a beat from Bolivia
In Hari Son's voice I heard, say hey dad I'm still missing ya
Singing "For You Blue," it ain't gossip nor trivia
In George's garden, was there a flowering plant named Clivia?

Lord Krishna came along for a spiritual ride
The Buddha jumped in the convertible, with a gong by his side
They drove around London in George's beautiful ferrari
Dhani singing, "For His Blue" a lovely musical tsunami

A big band sound I love Dhani's performance immense
His voice crackled at times, genetically related to the best
Being compared to you know who, Dhani, you've got a dad to divest
To the finish line you come, son of "Dark Horse," you passed the test

Ravi Shankar, I Am Missing You

You were always there to promote a cause
Assisting a novice Prabhupada in New York City
He didn't know the rules nor any laws
At George's side when he composed "My Sweet Lord" and "Isn't It a Pity"

Startled by Harrison's request to play sitar
Took hold of his hand while visiting places near and far
With George on David Frost's TV Show
Received a generous, "Bravo, Bravo"

Singing "Ride Rajbun" with Dhani and George
The frolicking rabbit dancing to and fro
"Chants of India" your masterpiece galore
Mantras from the Vedas, opened up our Hindu Door

It was your idea to relieve the people of Bangladesh
The first of its kind and absolutely the very best
George just made some phone calls to his friends
Did he phone the musician named John Tesh?

You were the father of George's 1974 Dark Horse Tour
Ali Akbar Khan, Alla Rakha, lasting forever to endure
Introducing the world to Indian Music and the sitar
Your continuing efforts earned The Lord's spiritual star

The Lord changed your clothes one day before twelve-twelve-twelve
The music of many legends came out of the woodwork and off the shelve
Nora Jones and Anoushka Shankar, your talented daughters
Your musical legacy, Krishna engaged and already hardened
No doubt you will be honored at Madison Square Garden

STILL WITH YOU

(Tribute to George Harrison)

Michael Geraghty 2005 (SOCAN)

When you cross the river
You know it's not forever
One day you will find me
Standing at your door

I have made the journey
There is no more yearning
I am with the one God
Who has made us all

Chorus:
So let Him into your soul
Give Him your warm hand to hold
And He will be there in your heart

When you feel that I'm gone
All you need do is sing my songs
And I will live on in your hearts

Still with you, I'm still with you

Do you really wonder
If I am rain or thunder
Or if I am flying
Out across the stars?

Let me tell you plainly
don't ramble on insanely
I am here in God's arms
I am not on Mars

Chorus

Bridge:
You, all of my life
You, every night
You, there in my arms
You, You

When you cross the river
You know it's not forever
One day you will find me
Standing at your door.

CHAPTER 2
Gurudas

Gurudas

Gurudas was a close friend of George Harrison for 33 years and has been a dear friend of mind for more than 3 years. With Mukunda Goswami and Shyamasundar, Gurudas introduced Krishna to The Beatles in late 1968. Olivia Harrison called them "the old gang" in *By His Example*, a book by Gurudas.

Gurudas took shelter of Srila Prabhupada as his spiritual master on April 07, 1967, becoming Prabhupada's initiated disciple. He was the first President of Sri Sri Radha Krishna Temple on Bury Place which later moved to Soho. Today, Krishna's home is Bhaktivedanta Manor in Radlett, the ISKCON Temple purchased by George Harrison in loving service for Krishna, his "My Sweet Lord."

Gurudas is "an ambassador of good will," said Bhaktivedanta "All Those Years Ago." Selected by The Founder Acharya to oversee the 6-year construction of the temple in Vrindavan, Gurudas continues to serve Krishna today. He shares his life's experiences with The Beatles and with A.C. Bhaktivedanta Swami Prabhupada on a worldwide lecture circuit. He also produces, directs, and promotes George Harrison Festivals, honoring the life of our friend George.

Gurudas has written a second edition to his popular 2004 book, *By His Example*, titled *The Wit and Wisdom of A.C. Bhaktivedanta Swami Prabhupada*. His latest work, *Love Medicine and Music*, is currently being published.

Gurudas encourages me to expand my Krishna consciousness by chanting, serving Krishna, and writing poetry. On many occasions I have referred to *Endless Beginnings*, his book of poetry, for inspiration. My retreats to ISKCON of Arizona at Tucson accentuate my desire to live a life with purpose guided by Krishna consciousness.

George Harrison icons began popping up on my desktop as Gurudas delivered over 30 photographs for *Sweet Serenity*. I asked him what was going on and he said, "Sometimes Krishna surprises on the upside."

Enjoy my Gurudas poetry! Each poem was written from the accompanying photograph while listening to George Harrison music.

Steven Leonard Schwartz

Chapter 2 Photograph Credits

Photographs Are the Property of Gurudas Unless Otherwise Noted

A Lifetime of Nectar

You give of yourself
So I could flourish
A lifetime of nectar
You were able to nourish

Krishna and Prabhupada
On the top of your list
They said go help Steven
You couldn't resist

A lifetime with George
A blissful synchronicity
Neither manufactured nor forged
Powered by Krishna's electricity

The Founder Acharya's protector
Loved from sea to shining sea
Lord Krishna Your mentor
Prabhupada's favorite devotee

BHAKTIVEDANTA!!

The world was his stage
Didn't matter what his age
He will always be our sage
BHAKTIVEDANTA!!

Confident and reassuring
Majestic and alluring
Fearless and unnerving
BHAKTIVEDANTA!!

The savior of us all
By His Example we stand tall
Devotees answer his call
BHAKTIVEDANTA!!

Possesses a chess master's vision
Sees all obstacles and opposition
Nothing stops him from his mission
BHAKTIVEDANTA!!

A pure heart and humility we're praising
He glides on sand as if walking on water – amazing
It's Krishna consciousness everyone is craving
BHAKTIVEDANTA!!

Our love for him is contagious
So much so our devotion is outrageous
Krishna high in the spiritual sky – he made us
BHAKTIVEDANTA!!

His flowing nectar is sweeter
As I read from *The Bhagavad-Gita*
I think I'll drink a liter
BHAKTIVEDANTA!!

Chanting Hare Krishna his face glows
As our love for Lord Krishna grows
Our friend, George Harrison, knows
BHAKTIVEDANTA!!

If you love Krishna it pleases him the most
Anywhere in the world including the United States coast
He teaches us the truth with no ego to boast
BHAKTIVEDANTA!!

Hear My Call

Open the ear within my heart
I don't need an invitation
Accept me from the start
I only need concentration

Wherever You are
It's never too far
However You may be
It's all right to me

I'm starvin' for Vrindavan
My heart aches as it hardens
Only six more miles on The Hare Krishna Highway
I'm tuning up my Harmonium Steinway

The Little Blue Boy is around the corner
No longer playing games like Little Jack Horner
All grown up He's a real heart warmer
He's Lord Krishna, a real transformer

Photograph © Gauravani

I NEVER WALK ALONE

Gurudas is the ISKCON Founder Acharya's watchful protector
Providing surveillance and guidance for the "Man with the Scepter"
Prabhupada walks on water like gliding on sand
I execute his demands like no one else can

I have his front and back from every side and angle
Never for a split second do I ever get wrangled
I complete the scene way before the actors arrive
My life serving Krishna ensures Prabhupada's dream stays alive

Thinking on my feet while chanting sixteen rounds
Being Krishna strong yet Radha sleek, I keep you in bounds
My life lives within the pages of your *Bhagavad-Gita*
My life gives to Krishna and no one is sweeter

I'm here – every second, every minute, every hour of every day
I'm there – every week, every month, every year in every possible way
Even though you've left your body for a new suit of clothes
Your servant, Gurudas, "Never Walks Alone," as his love for you ever grows

IWO JIMA KRISHNA

Gurudas just called me he said stop the presses
To serve Krishna with love is what he stresses
IWO JIMA Krishna in Czechoslovakia we just raised the flag
Any love less than the ultimate maximum is “Kind of a Drag”

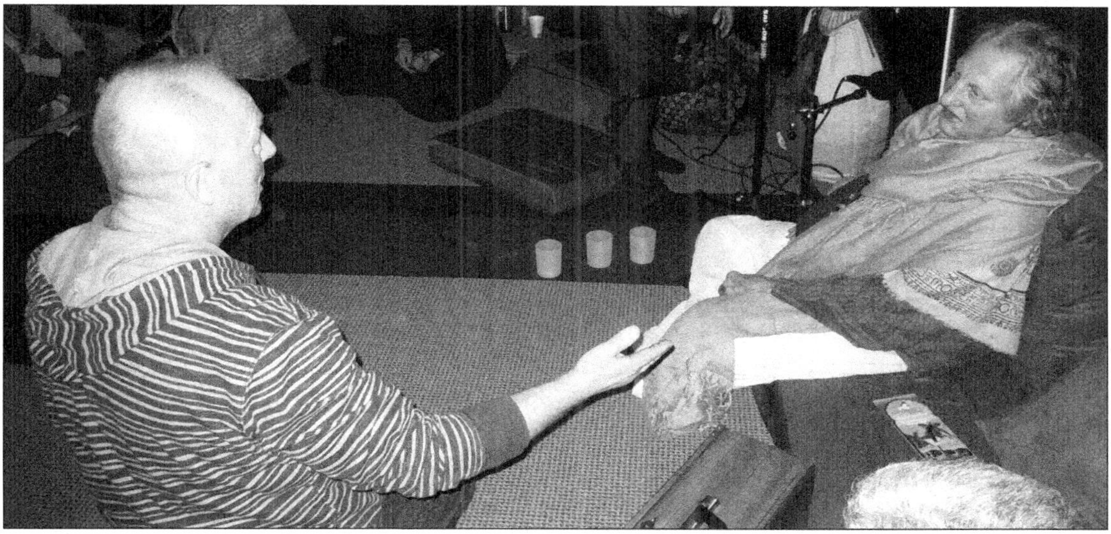

Krishna Stronger

Surrender unto Me everything you own
Release your burdens to Krishna, I know you're not alone
Whatever you are mourning it's not worthy of the grief
Search in your suffering, you will find absolute relief

Take stock of your life, what I have and what I have not
Only what you need to get by is required on the spot
Remaining equitable and balanced is Krishna's ultimate test
The answer is to be Krishna conscious equally in happiness and distress

Krishna, purify my senses it's my mind's consensus
Give me the knowledge to break through the material world fences
Let me come back to You please accept my association
Enrich my life, Krishna, with Your spiritual realization

Krishna, You are my everything be my automatic pilot
I just saw Elvis parachute, there will be no jailhouse riot
My love turned on the starter, let's fly together farther and longer
I gave George a first class seat, so he too can become "Krishna Stronger"

Lift Me Up

"Your True Love" is what I'm lookin' for
Not like it was with that other band before
When You're ready for me, I'm still standing "Behind That Locked Door"
Through Your open window, Krishna, I see Your beauty more and more

Listening to Carl Perkins and his Memphis rockabilly beat
Makes me "Glad All Over" and lifts me right up out of my seat
Playing that Sun Records sound as Carl does so fine
I'm almost "Knocking On Heaven's Door" with visions of You from "Cloud 9"

You came from Vrindavan with Your heart on Your sleeve
You're everybody's Lord, including me, Bhakta Steve
I'll choose You every opportunity I have sight unseen
Don and Phil sang about You every time they had a dream

My feelings for You are real, they will never be concealed
I'm telling You the truth, "My Love" will always be revealed
I admire Bob Dylan but Carl Perkins takes me to a higher note
You will never hear George Harrison say, Krishna, well "Honey Don't"

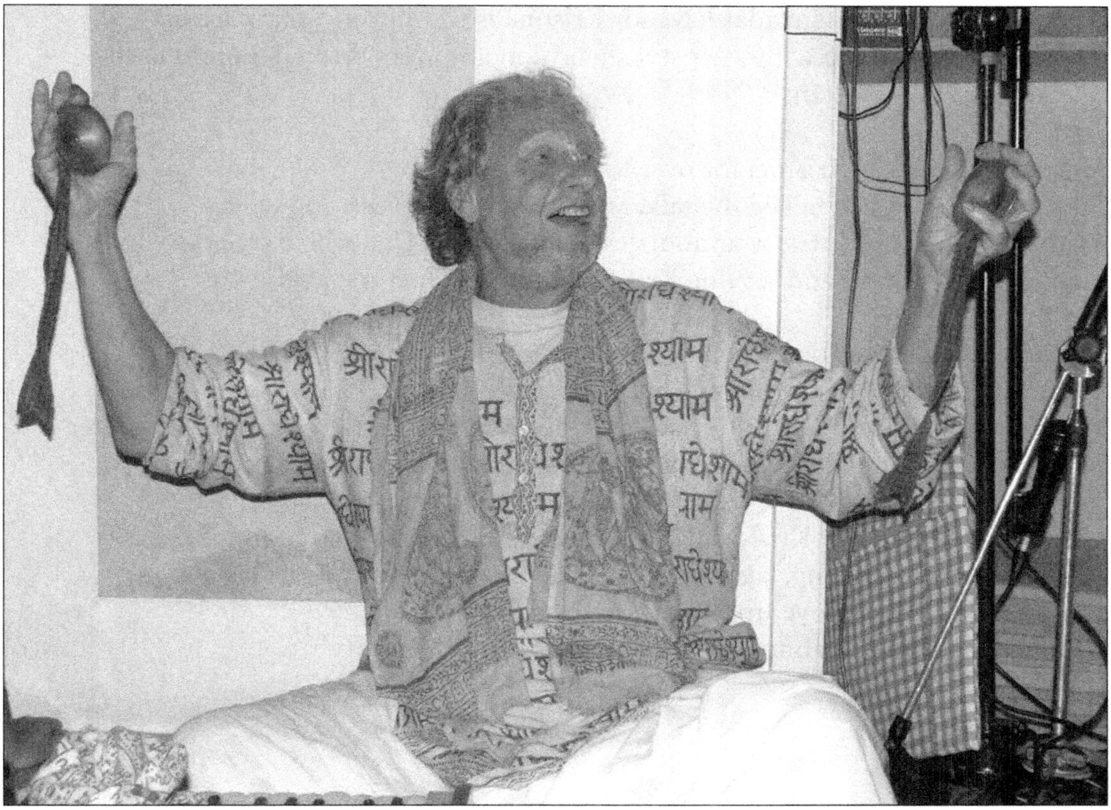

My Guru Friend

He's a grown-up kid just like you and me
Livin' the life he's been given with Krishna vitality
The truth be told his story is very interesting to me
Gurudas opened the Krishna door to Harrison, Starr, Lennon, and McCartney

Initiated with his wife Yamuna in the spring of nineteen sixty-seven
Ventured across the pond to expand their Krishna consciousness twenty-four-seven
With Mukunda and Shyamasundar they encountered the mersey beat
First Temple President at Bury Place, surely put a smile on Krishna's face

The rooftop above Apple Records became The Hare Krishna Garrison
"The Hare Krishna Maha Mantra" and "Govinda" were recorded by friend George Harrison

The love George and Gurudas have for Krishna is way beyond comparison
The devotees were hip with their stylish fashion and were loved in London as
American Samaritans

Gurudas has served Krishna for over forty years
He's walked the walk, talked the talk, and shed blood, sweat, and tears
With a lions's roar, Gurudas announces, Krishna's the One who made me whole
Continuously loving and serving Krishna is his only lifetime goal

Krishna is his "Brite Star" when at home or traveling afar
With "My Sweet Lord" by his side his life is never ajar
I love Krishna's smile, admire Krishna's style, every mile on my Krishna odometer
With Bhaktivedanta, I've walked with the Lord a lotta Krishna kilometers

Gurudas loves the way Krishna dances when George sings "Something"
Krishna is truly amazing, keeps me believing, and makes my heart sing
Krishna is my "True Love" may we never be apart
The moment I met Prabhupad, I knew it right from the start

The Guru Man

His name is known throughout ISKCON
He truly is one of a kind
The Guru of all Gurus
Gurudas is Bhaktivedanta's greatest find

Guru'd out, NO WAY!!
His Krishna love don't take no holiday
He's having too much fun
Chanting with George on the harmonium

On the anniversary of George's passing
My love for George is still surpassing
George said, never give up, never stop trying
Gurudas keeps Hari's guitar forever smiling

His beginnings are endless
"Any Road" takes him there
Gurudas is not friendless
He's loved by devotees everywhere

You can call him Roger
A San Francisco fan not fond of the Dodgers
Been around the block, a stodgy veteran codger
Krishna provides shelter for the seventy-two-year-old lodger

Spreading Prabhupada's message, he's serving
Guru-ing around the world, he's unnerving
He's Krishna tried and true, deserving
A.C. Bhaktivedanta's dream, he's preserving

He's Krishna's man in the middle
George strums the ukulele as he plays the fiddle
Looking for souls to make a spiritual change
Traversing the globe Krishna's always in range

From Prabhupada's wisdom he's absorbed every sample
Learned from his leadership, *By His Example*
A dear friend of George Harrison on his own accord
Gurudas loves to hear George sing "My Sweet Lord"

The Three Krishnateers

(Gurudas, Mukunda & George)

There's no need to "Imagine"
We're "All Together Now"
"The Long and Winding Road"
Ended in Friar Park Henley, somehow

No longer a "Nowhere Man"
Not "Tangled Up in Blue"
What a reunion trip it's been
I'm a Krishnateer, Lord, just "Love Me Do"

"Walk This Way" to The Three Krishnateers
Chant and pray, Krishna knows your tears
"Give Me Love (Give Me Peace on Earth)"
"My Sweet Lord," I'm on Your turf

I'm feeling "Good Vibrations"
No frustrations only elations
Pure devotion and "Sweet Emotion"
Bhaktivedanta Manor is Krishna dancing to "The Loco-Motion"

Krishna, "I'm a Believer"
Srila Prabhupad is my "Dream Weaver"
You're "Always on My Mind"
Thank You, Thank You, You're so kind

"No Matter What" Your love is here to stay
I continue to serve You "Day After Day"
"You're In My Heart," "You're My Best Friend"
Like Hari George, You will be with me right to the end

The Trutnov Open Air Music Festival

In the Czech Republic, many attend the Krishna festival at Trutnov abound
They "Come Together" to hear George Harrison's music and revel in his guitar sound
From miles around just as Rick Nelson sings in his "Travelin' Man"
Walking on foot or driving by car, Krishna is everybody's "Far East Man"

From every town and village any lineage and every sect
Hearing Gurudas George-speak leaves us spellbound in any dialect
George's way of knowing and flowing Krishna's words into his lyrics
Keeps Prabhupada's *Bhagavad-Gita* alive and well as Bhaktivedanta elevates our spirits

The meaning behind George's music is a celebrated Krishna symphony
Our "Dark Horse," the music's source, is a flower to the bee jubilee
Gurudas tells many a George story as he spins some Harrison vinyl
His "True Love" found, his life fulfilled, "Still Crazy After All These Years" it's Krishna smart and final

Gurudas smiles with Krishna charm and raises his arms, so comfortably
Krishna is free, available to you and me, there's never any admission fee
Oh what a feeling, the Om flag is breezing, I am always Krishna believing
The "Ding Dong Ding Dong" bell is ringing, I am never Krishna leaving

The Winning Move

The winning move is to not play the game
Chant Hare Krishna and you will become tame
Purification deters the taste for materialization
Change your life for a brand new salvation

Ukulele Guru

Do it for you and your beloved, too
Smile all the way through, sing "Ukulele Guru"
A strum here and a strum there
The Lord loves you, "Here, There and Everywhere"

Discover yourself, never give up your role
Do it for your soul, the Lord made you whole
Put on your bowler, wear it to the side or at an angle
The Lord loves you, "Mr. Bojangles"

Open the Lord's gate, you have a reserved seat so don't be late
His love is pure, He's the real thing, He ain't no surrogate
The Lord's devotion is going to carry you through
"Walk With The Lord," He's "Devoted To You"

George said, never give up, never stop trying
Roy G. Biv, it's time to live, so keep on climbing
"Haven't Got Time for the Pain," be strong and remain
Always remember John F. Kennedy's eternal flame

CHAPTER 3

Lord Krishna

(Introducing Yogi Girl Yogi Guy)

This is All Possible by the
GRACE
of
Lord Sri Krishna
&
their Guru Dev
Gopal Krishna Goswami Maharaj

Rukmini-Priya Devi Dasi
Painter, Designer, Jewelry Maker

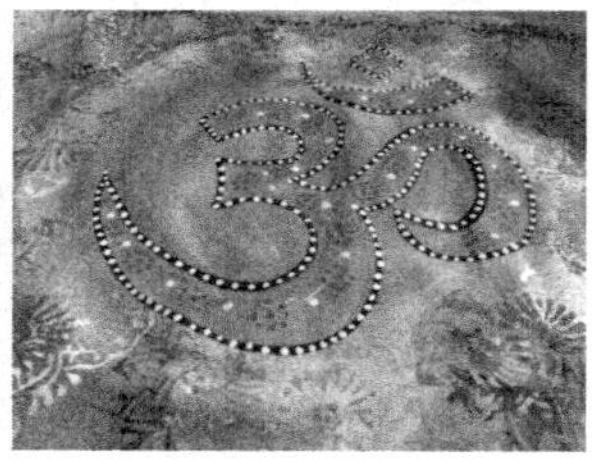

yogi girl yogi guy™

A Lifestyle brand.

Clothing & accessories that reflect a sense inner peace and awakens your soul from within. Yogic Urban chic mixed with a California laid back vibe.

Worn by everyone-everywhere!

Find Us on Facebook, Twitter, & Instagram and **remember, it's never too late, to find your Om.® with YGYG Apparel & Accessories!**
www.YogigirlYogiguy.com or www.YGYGApparel.com

Chapter 3 Photograph Credits

Photographs Are the Property of Steven Leonard Schwartz
Unless Otherwise Noted

A Krishna Journey

Krishna sent me on a journey to experience life on the go
I probably reached a point where You desired me to travel to and fro
I'm at a level where I seem to understand more of it all
Since removing the darkness from my sight, I'm walking straight and standing tall

The pathway up ahead has some visible twists and turns
Because of You, Oh Krishna, it's not that much of a concern
You keep my ears wide open and help me hold my tongue
While listening to someone's opinion and hearing their mouth run

Something of importance may be said that I must be able to construe
The patience You provide, Oh Krishna, helps me to follow better, yes it's true
Keep me within Your depth of field, I desire to always be in the photograph with You
Krishna, Your will carries me through, I'm in good hands because of You

A Letter To Krishna

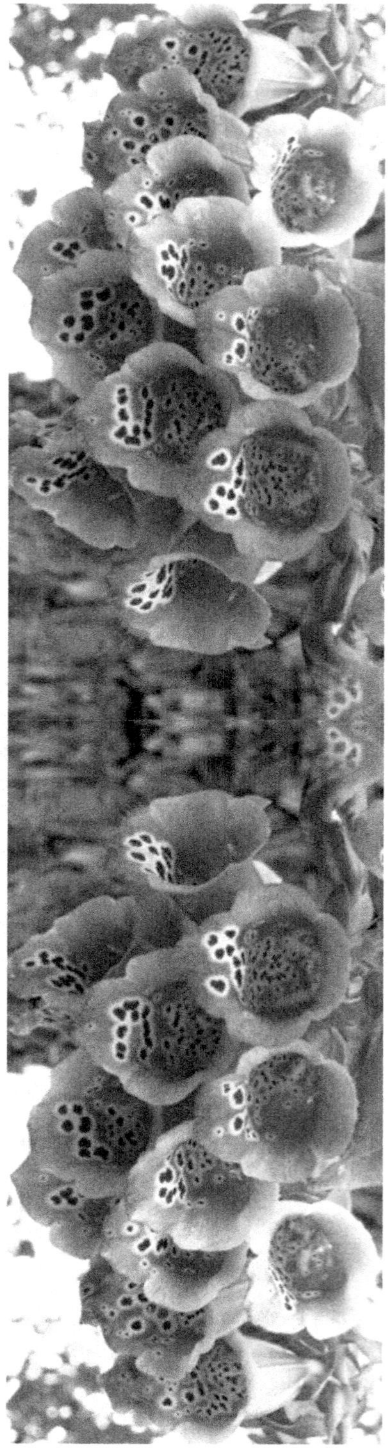

Krishna, where have you been
I'm not feeling You within
My heart is empty and hollow
Please fill it with joy and remove the sorrow

Gotta get away from it all
The order is way too tall
"It's All Too Much"
Too sensitive to the touch

The line is busy to get to You
It's too cloudy I can't see the view
My patience is wearing thin
I'm breaking down from within

The stoplight changed and it said to go
My artery's blocked, there's very little flow
Moving at a snail's pace I'm gonna have heartache
Not enough patience and time, there's too much at stake

Send me to a place that's innocent and pure
Within Your reach so I can endure
Somewhere I can be myself and be totally sure
Certainly Krishna will help find a cure

It's not where you've been
But where you're going
Not the strength of the wind
But the direction it's blowing

I've got the lead on the pack to attain Your love
Post position one chosen from up above
I'm heading for the finish along the rail
My love for You, Krishna will never curtail

A Little Bit of Krishna

I want Krishna now and I always will
"A Little Bit of Krishna" certainly fits the bill
Lift me up through the rarefied air
I want to be with You Lord, in a higher atmosphere

The more I chant the closer You appear
You're True Blue Krishna, You really, really, care
You lend a helping hand whenever I'm around
I call out Your name and I'm Hare Krishna found

I want You to see, Lord, that I'm Krishna strong
Singing Your song I definitely belong
"Got My Mind Set On You" let's set a date to meet
Now I know why George called You "Sweet"

Krishna is the One I really desire
Your eternal love never expires
Lord, You always spark my spiritual flame
Without Krishna in my life, it just wouldn't be the same

All I Need Is Krishna

Upside down and inside out
Krishna is My Lord, there is no doubt
Downside up and outside in
Krishna loves me from within

Right side left and left side right
Being with Krishna is dynamite
High in the sky or low to the ground
Krishna is the best friend I've ever found

No matter how I feel
Happy, sad, depressed or sick
Loving You, Krishna, keeps me real
I know it can happen very quick

I close my eyes and think of You
Automatically You appear in view
You come to me with a subtle grace
Welcoming me in a loving embrace

Makes no difference my ethnicity
You love me for my simplicity
Krishna, You don't require any publicity
Everyone loves You for Your authenticity

Krishna, Krishna, You're all I need
I think of You and I will succeed
Keep me alive and ticking and in the lead
Stay by my side and never leave

Be Like Krishna

Krishna fades into the spiritual sunset
Nothing to remember nothing to forget
Like a running stream His mind is clear
Don't need don't want, He makes it all disappear

Krishna walks away from anything
Detached from all material things
Neither lifts an eyebrow, nor blinks an eye
We can be more like Krishna if we really want to try

Chant a bit more and see what's in store
It's what you value and what you stand for
A little more love is what Krishna admires
Follow the *Bhagavad-Gita*, that's what He desires

The thoughts in my head with the dark and the light
At the end of the rainbow is a wonderful delight
The clouds blow away, they're nowhere to be found
Nothing but blue sky and the Hare Krishna chanting sound

Be There Krishna

Krishna, I don't know what I'd do without You
You watch over me and make sure I'm all right
No more attachments, no maya harassments
Bhaktivedanta says You're outta sight

Being with You, Lord Krishna, makes me glad
You keep me mostly happy and minimize the sad
You're the One who changed my life
I love to hear You play Your flute and fife

We have so much fun chanting Hare Krishna
George says You're "My Sweet Lord"
Always be with me, My Beloved, so blissfully
You're the Lord everyone can afford

Please follow me, Lord, everywhere I go
I know You're there even if Your face don't show
I feel Your presence by the deeds You do
Sometimes I gotta work harder to hear You say, I love you

Dancing Krishna

Upside down and inside out
Krishna knows what it's all about
It's all right to have some fun
When you share it with a special someone

Krishna's there under the lights
Struttin' with Radha his girlfriend every night
Dancing shoes on lookin' like a dream
Krishna's a disco dancing machine

Now Krishna knows all the moves
In his tuxedo He really grooves
Krishna dances the two-step and the tango
Watch Him as He does the fandango

"Dancing with the Stars"
With host Tom Bergeron
Contestants Radha and Krishna
Turn the Hindu heat on

Their moves are really out of sight
The couple scored perfect tens for the night
Outstanding applause from the judges
Their opponents in awe held no grudges

The audience cheered bravo and wanted more
For Radha and Krishna here comes an encore
The Hare Krishna Band came marching in the door
The couple already knew what was in store

We're going to perform a famous line dance
An Indian favorite everybody's gonna prance
Here's A.C. Prabhupada leading the way
As his Krishna band begins to play

Mr. George Harrison on lead guitar
His melodic chords take us away real far
He's here to entertain us until the cows come home
Balarama's going to lead us to the Hare Krishna zone

Everyone follows as Krishna shows us the way
The Hare Krishna Maha Mantra is the hit of the day
Chanting and dancing in the television studio
The crowd is Krishnad Out after an hour or so

The producer says it's almost time to go
Prabhupada says oh no we won't go
We'll leave on my terms when I say so
The *Bhagavad-Gita* to everyone, every seat, every row

A wonderful night with Radha and Krishna, galore
Prabhupada is escorted to his Watseka Avenue Temple to restore
Until the next time when we're together for more
Another tale from the book of Lord Krishna Lore

George Harrison's Lord

My name is Krishna
I'm Prabhupad's machine
George Harrison's Lord
I'm everybody's dream

Come to the Temple
You're gonna be heard
Chant along with Krishna
You know the words

Hare Krishna Hare Krishna
Krishna Krishna Hare Hare
Hare Rama Hare Rama
Rama Rama Hare Hare

Over thousands of years
I've seen many people
Eyes flowing tears
From Krishna's steeple

I know who you are
And where you've been
If you've traveled far
Or lost from within

Have faith in Krishna
That's all you gotta do
George sang about me
"Got My Mind Set On You"

Let me feel your heart (from)
"Behind That Locked Door"
Love Krishna from the start
Neither rich nor poor

Spiritual attraction
Krishna satisfaction
It won't take long
Here's Buddha's gong

From the Spiritual Sky
The highest level of the high
A.C.'s private eye
Will never say good-bye

High Flying Krishna

Krishna, get me through the day
I don't want to be alone anymore
Although You're thousands of miles away
Your love is always right next door

A loving deity like You is so hard to find
Your mellifluous voice fills the canyons in my mind
Your chanting echoes louder and faster
Because Krishna, You are My Spiritual Master

The Tucson hills and valleys silhouette
A view from the Krishna Temple I will never forget
My perpetual love for You has my Krishna kite high flying
No matter how windy, Your love is pacifying

Krishna, all I want to do is hold Your hand
I'm at Your service just give the command
Please show me the way to Your home today
I desire You more each and every day

It's no surprise, Krishna, You're forever on my mind
Nobody's like You, You're a once in a lifetime find
You are the One love that I've really got
Would do anything for You, without a second's thought

If It's Spiritual It's Krishna

Reach past it with your outstretched arms
Beyond its border there is no harm
Beauty and goodness are on the other side
Travel with Krishna on a magic carpet ride

The Bhagavad-Gita contains thousands of purports
Bhaktivedanta detaches you from attachments of all sorts
A Prabhupad original book with no imitations
Your mind harbors the only limitations

Prabhupad purports thoughts more infinite
Understand his meaning and really get into it
Absorb the message sent from above
There for your taking signed Krishna with love

Krishna, You suddenly appear when I need You the most
You never cry and You never boast
You are the One I love the most
Whether I'm on the Atlantic or the Pacific coast

In My Life

Krishna gives me choices to help me become stronger
I want to love You Lord harder and for much longer
When my mind wanders away You're always within reach
Any George Harrison song and I'm reminded of everything You teach

Many times Krishna, all I see is darkness instead of light
Open my eyes wider so my vision encompasses Your full sight
Krishna, I'm not the only one seeking out Your sweet nectar
In Tucson's Botanical Garden, a butterfly is not just a paying spectator

Krishna, let this moment in my life be all that it can be, so I can make the world believe-in
That with Your love I can do anything I want, something nobody else can achieve-in
Unlock the mechanism to Your heart space, let me enter and never let me be leavin'
A single thread of Your love connects me to You above, and my name is Bhakta Steven

In The Midst of The Middle With Krishna

Don't need no phone
There's no one to talk to
No steps – no stairs
There's no place to walk to

Everwatchful – everknowing
You are always by my side
Everpresent – everlasting
Your love can shift the ocean's tide

Oh, when I'm here
All I need is Krishna
It's been so long
I don't wanna miss Ya

You give me calm
You send me peace
That's where I wanna be
On the path to A.C. Prabhupad
The sweetest serenity

It Matters To Me

Oh Krishna, it matters to me
I want to love You with the sweetest serenity
Being Your servant every day and night
Let's read *The Bhagavad-Gita* till morning light

Oh Krishna, anytime I reach out to You
My number's on speed dial, I always get through
The message You send I'll never forget
Your view of life is my spiritual sunset

Oh Krishna, the maya hex has passed me by
With its GPS disabled, there's nowhere to spy
A rolling stone gathers no moss
There's no map, no compass, it's definitely lost

A foot of fresh snow fell in just a few hours
I can't see the time on the clock's ivory towers
My candle flickers as You explain a purport's reason
You will understand the meaning just keep reading and believing

It's Krishna Time

I desire to connect with You all of the time
No operator assistance don't need a dime
Stay with me always there is never any rent
From the spiritual sky Your love is heaven sent

I want to serve You every week
And pray at the base of Your lotus feet
Reading *The Bhagavad-Gita* is my Krishna drink
It quenches my spiritual thirst and energizes my mind to think

It pleases me to please You every day
I adore You immensely stay with me and never go away
Our love's not for sale it will never be returned
A permanent purchase all receipts have been burned

I really need to be with You every second
At Your service whenever You beckon
My caped crusader and spiritual hero
Without You, Lord, my life would be worth zero

Just Krishna

Just phone Him up it's easy to connect
Krishna takes my call long distance or collect
The line is crystal clear it's like He's right here
Krishna is available to answer any day of the year

Knowing Krishna is My Lord is a wonderful present
Krishna lends me a hand His voice is very pleasant
Reading from *The Bhagavad-Gita* or anything with a Prabhupad label
Fills my heart with Krishna and I'm a lot more stable

I'm happy Krishna likes having me around
Chanting Hare Krishna in stereo surround sound
Listening to "My Sweet Lord" on compact cassettes
Krishna resembles Ganesha as He never forgets

Krishna keeps my spiritual dream alive
Under His guidance I prosper and thrive
Krishna and me we ain't talkin no jive
I passed His course now I'm Krishnatized

Krishna Birthday Blues

Krishna Krishna take me with You
I don't wanna be blue today
Krishna Krishna show me the way
To the place I wanna be right away

I want You so much
You've got Srila Prabhupada's touch
You have the vision to see
What's going on with me

The path I take today determines my tomorrow
The road to You leads to joy not to sorrow
Krishna Krishna so many don't get through
I have a straight line to You whenever

Krishna Krishna I'm glad You chose me too
I'm happy to be Your servant forever
Our connection is so direct
I'll never call collect

My love for You will never sever
Teach me to deal with all that is real
I wanna live on an even keel
That's my endeavor

Krishna Bound

Right at this moment I'm feeling peaceful within
An overwhelming compassion is causing me to grin
Like Dylan on "Nashville Skyline" as Bob tips his brim
"Just For Today," it's nice not being on the outside looking in

Everything's in order nothing's out of line
I've reached a place I can call mine
The rain has stopped the sky's filled with sunshine
I need to be patient cause it's gonna take some precious time

A void of anxiety has my feet on the ground
Not hyper nor reactive just stable and sound
Not going in circles my love has been found
My cruise control is set, I'm Hare Krishna bound

George Harrison is singing, "Give Me Love (Give Me Peace On Earth)"
He's a constant reminder how much Krishna is worth
George dedicated his life looking for the answers to the cause
He received in return Olivia's love and Krishna's applause

Krishna Clear

I have to say how I really feel
Or I won't be honest with myself
And be Krishna real

I've got to speak what's on my mind
Or I won't be true to myself
And be Krishna kind

I must see what my vision unwinds
In the optical nerves of my mind
Or I will become Krishna blind

Filtering every word I hear
Certifying the message is Krishna clear
If I seem not to agree
I have the right to Krishna disagree

The waters are sometimes dark and murky
Consider the source and the history
Then it truly ain't no mystery
My Krishna talk is crystal clear to me

To have my Krishna consciousness equal in happiness and distress
If I can do this then I'm a Krishna success, 'cause I passed His test
Oh what a feeling to always be in Krishna balance
Then my atomic structure will be in Krishna valence

Krishna Is Here To Stay

I struggled for years
Shed waterfalls of tears
The outpouring from my eyes
Flooded the spiritual skies

It's easy to turn back
When you've been attacked
The clear view to Your love
Just became opaque
My arteries have hardened
My heart sincerely aches

Stay with me Krishna
Please don't leave
No Muhammad Ali
Don't float like a butterfly
Don't sting like a bee
Don't dodge and weave
Remember George Harrison's "If You Believe"

Photosynthesize the sunlight
Orange, red, and yellow
The leaves disintegrate and fall, but
Your leaves, Krishna, never leave

Keep my eyes wide open
Don't want to become Krishna blind
Material world dealing and be coping
You're the One who's on my mind

Every breath I take
Every step I amble
Your love is inhaled
Never a Las Vegas gamble

Whether You're in my hood
Or a few miles away
Serving You, Krishna, is very good
You're my Lord every day

Krishna Love

I look You in the eye
I find You everyplace
My connection to the spiritual sky
You make sense of the human race

Don't have to jump through hoops
No need to pull a lever
Don't require military troops
To know I want to serve You forever

Don't have to ring a bell
No need to drive too far
It's not difficult to tell
You are my shining star

It's very easy to keep believin'
You call me Bhakta Steven
Makes no difference what the season
Krishna loves me for any reason

Krishna OH MY Krishna

Krishna OH MY Krishna
You right me when I'm wrong
You help me sing Your song
Keep me in Your sacred space, the place where I belong
George was right, it takes too long
Krishna OH MY Krishna

Krishna MY LORD Krishna
The Bhagavad-Gita I want to learn
Purports relating to me I must discern
Gotta change my ways before the next turn
The most difficult detachments are the toughest to burn
Krishna MY LORD Krishna

Krishna MY LOVE Krishna
The day You entered my heart
I loved You from the start
Your love cannot be bought
It has to be earned by service on the spot
Krishna MY LOVE Krishna

Krishna I PRAY Krishna
Help me make it through the day
Keep me on the correct pathway
Please don't leave and go away
I want You today and everyday
Krishna I PRAY Krishna

Krishna MY GUARDIAN Krishna
When it's dark at night show me
Your light shining bright
Give me strength to defeat my enemies tonight
It's time I start smiling and eliminate the fright
My eyes realize it's going to be all right
Krishna MY GUARDIAN Krishna

Krishna on My Mind

Through Prabhupad's accord
I know You are my Lord
Sometimes You handle me like a used 74 Ford
Make me broken hearted by being an absentee landlord

Lift me up when I don't hear You chanting
When I have fallen I'm raving and ranting
Unconditionally You make my heart sing
You are completely free of anything and everything

From the outside looking in
You can see the inside looking out
Please don't make me "Twist and Shout"
Krishna, I just wanna be more devout

Chanting Your Name it's one of a kind
Serving You with all the energy I can find
Always want to be Krishna inclined
I want to live my life in a Krishna state of mind

Krishna Rap

This song's about Krishna
My right hand man
He's by my side
No matter where I am

If I'm travelin' far
Or close to home
Krishna's with me
Wherever I roam

He's at my job
Working "9 to 5"
Like John Travolta
Keeps me "Stayin' Alive"

If the road of life
Seems all uphill
As Krishna says
It sometimes will

Take the easy path
Not the one that's harder
And get advice
From my girlfriend, Radha

Or use a lifeline
And phone Ganesha
My elephant friend
He'll release ya

When the daily grind's
Too much a chore
Take a trip to India
Visit Bangalore

Krishnaland/Krishnatown

The world rests on the palms of Krishna's hands
Live your life following His commands
It doesn't matter where I am
Because I'm standing tall in Krishnaland

My daily life is in His control
He is the keeper of my very soul
Ensures my spirit is safe and whole
Taught George Harrison to play rock and roll

Takes me higher and higher as a great diety should
He's admired by everyone in my neighborhood
Knows my history the bad and the good
From childhood to adulthood, Krishna eyes my livelihood

Krishna's stature and grace is stronger than any sword
He can direct the flow of the Mississippi River or a Norway fjord
Prefers the Pontiac Grand Am over any car by Ford
Inspired George to write "My Sweet Lord"

Call waiting or busy signal I'll invest the dime
And stand in the phone booth come rain or come shine
I would love to serve You until the end of time
Your servant, George, wrote "I'd Have You Anytime"

Chant Hare Krishna, Hare Krishna, and I can be found
With Radha and Krishna on the merry-go-round
Smiling and happy, flying high off the ground
From sunrise to sundown I'm singing His sound
Chanting the Lord's holy name in Krishnatown

Krishnatized

Krishna knows what my eyes have seen
He discerns who I am and where I've been
One thing is certain I've definitely realized
I love Krishna so much I've been Krishnatized

I joined the club, no admission fee
No membership card, no photo ID
Don't have to take a tour of the facility
My free access never expires because Krishna loves me

Be yourself, but always think of Me
Feel peace inside, let Me relax your personality
Treat others respectfully, that's what I want to see
Live a simple life with grace and Krishnality

My Daily Dose of Krishna

Lord Krishna never stops giving
He's my twenty-four hour emergency call
Krishna's thoughtful guidance keeps me living
Don't need Ganesha unless I stumble and fall

My daily dose of Krishna is a spiritual transfusion, an unlimited recharge
Jump start my heart with Krishna there's never any service charge
Keep Krishna's motor running I'll pay for the gasoline
I'm synchronized with Krishna, no attachments ever seen

I don't have to enlist 'cause Krishna's ready for battle
He's ever present for me and for you
Wearing Prabhupad's uniform Krishna never gets rattled
His devotion to Radha is true blue

Listening to "My Sweet Lord" on a lily pad
George reinforces my Krishna connection
Krishna is the best friend I've ever had
I will admire and serve Him with the utmost affection

My Krishna Connection

Just awoken from my overnight's sleep
A new day beginning at Krishna's lotus feet
The back burner of my mind's been on auto pilot
Kept it warm so Krishna could realize it

Never turned it off there's a good connection
Don't wanna reboot and lose Krishna's convection
I love it when my "Krishnatic" energy is flowing
I'm ready to serve Krishna wherever I'm going

It doesn't matter where I am
It makes no difference how fast or slow
I'm walking on the treadmill of life
The more I see Krishna the further I go

Krishna transcended me to another place in time
It's very peaceful here, the clock stopped it's chime
Krishna, I'm ready to sign on the dotted line
Give me the contract make Krishna mine

Out The Door With Krishna

I'm going to walk with You, Krishna, right out the front door
Put your arm around Me, Steven, don't take it no more
It's obvious to Me 'cause Krishna knows the score
Your employer doesn't realize how valuable you've been before

You performed your job without looking for praise
Quite well being short staffed over 18 months, that's a lot of days
Your Khapra Beetle find was worthy of outstanding merit
But knowing the government as I do, they just buried it

The time has come to cleanse your soul
The clock is ticking for you to become whole
Thank you Krishna for fulling my spiritual desire
I chanted the entire time, Krishna, You really inspire

Pot of Gold

I'm a fish out of water left alone on the sand
Not knowing which way to turn in Never Neverland
Bring me home, Krishna, I'm stranded on the beach
I'm a solitary man isolated, distant from your reach

Krishna, I quench my thirst for Your sweet nectar above
Your "Pot of Gold" was delivered by a snow white dove
Everything that's happened occurred for a reason
The harder I search the more I'm Krishna believing

Krishna, when I find You it will just be the beginning
I want You by my side, support me while I'm living
Don't let me be a top out of control continuously spinning
"Not the Batman's Riddler, always joking and grinning"

A journey of a lifetime begins with one step
The more faith I have the further I'll get
My mind's channeled on You the satellite radio is set
My seat's confirmed on Krishna's spiritual jet

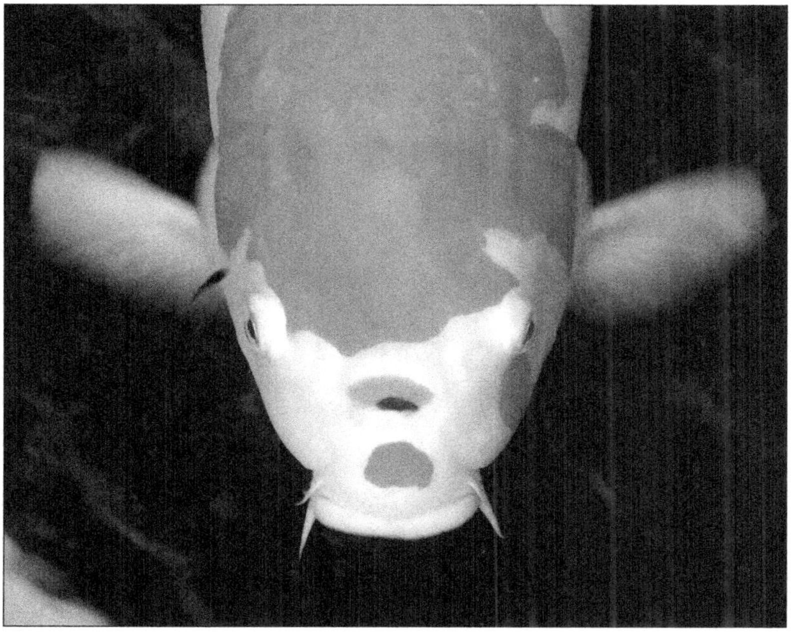

The Elevator

Krishna, take me to a higher level
The elevator only goes so high
I see You through the glass that's beveled
There's no button to push for the spiritual sky

Krishna, teach me what I need to learn
So my heart can direct connect with You
Your outpouring of love is what I yearn
Open my eyes and provide a better view

Krishna, stay with me and read Prabhupada's scripture
The prescription of Our love is a congenial mixture
Electrify my life with Your spiritual white light
A special relationship that makes me feel all right

To Krishna On My 56th Birthday

Krishna, You catch my stare
You come from anywhere
Your companionship is grand
Don't need a command

No need for an eruption
They'll be no disruption
You flow direct to my heart
We will never be apart

Krishna, I see You face to face
I desire to serve in every space
I am humbled by Your style and grace
Krishna be with me everyplace

It makes no difference where You walk on earth
Be it Rodeo Drive or Fifth Avenue

Krishna consciousness is present in all of us
It just needs regular maintenance by The Little Boy Blue

No need to give Krishna an address
Or a key to unlock Your Door
Krishna knows where You are if You love him
He's got a master to every domicile, business, and store

Krishna is the most important factor in my life
He loves His devotees including me very much
Everything is becoming Krishnatized
Krishna has that mystical, magical touch

Diamonds are inexpensive, jewelers scream it's corrupt
The wealthiest king's fortune is bankrupt
Gold loses its shiny luster, silver can't fetch a cup of coffee in Perth
Compared to the innumerable value Krishna is worth

Happy Birthday, Bhakta Steve
Stay with Krishna and never leave
The Tucson devotees will help if there's more to achieve
Keep chanting Hare Krishna and you will believe

Walk Away

Stop spreading all those lies
Krishna don't believe your alibis
He sees through the disguise
Blindness in my eyes has me mesmerized

Maya makes me feel
Like I have to run away
Saps my energy and my appeal
Can't get away from its material way

I can't go nowhere else,
'cause I'm running away from a part of myself
I take it with me wherever I go
Maya, you ain't part of Krishna's show

No more desiring material provisions
Krishna's performing my personal exorcism
I see clearly now because of my newfound vision
Krishna set me free from the material world prison

Tonight in Vrindavan I'm Krishna dreaming
No longer alone no more maya deceiving
You're my Lord forevermore You encompass my soul
My Lord Krishna,You play a huge role

It takes a special reality to really feel at peace
I signed onto Krishna's team with a lifelong lease
Prabhupad gave me a book from his personal valise
Autographed to Bhakta Steven it was a lovely piece

Walk away from the daily biz
The carbonation that makes coca cola fizz
Walk this way to what's breathing and lives
Open your heart to "The Bhagavad Gita as it is"

CHAPTER 4

The Founder Acharya

A. C. Bhaktivedanta Swami Prabhupada

Chapter 4 Photograph Credits

Photographs Are the Property of Steven Leonard Schwartz
Unless Otherwise Noted

Dedication to Prabhupada

You guide me through the maze of life
From the spiritual sky on a flute with a fife
Many miles to travel on Srila Prabhupada's path
Bhagavad-Gita in hand I can chant, smile, and laugh

Rewind my mind to any chapter and verse
Play the tape of the "Gita" there's no need to rehearse
Keep my heart open wide as Krishna's love has been found
"The Hare Krishna Maha Mantra" has me chanting high off the ground

Stay by my side Krishna, I love You more than ever
"Chant and Be Happy" it gets better and better
Don't know the obstacles lurking round the bend
Krishna's here to catch me instead of free falling to the end

My journey continues new scripture to learn
Rethink how I'm living old habits to burn
Be calm and peaceful curtail my emotion
Don't wanna be a tidal wave causing commotion in the ocean

You give me strength to carry on and show me wrong from right
You are a beacon in my every breath and keep the light shining bright
Muhammad Ali said he was the greatest of all time, but
Was he ever was introduced to Prabhupada and Krishna, The Divine

Keep Moving Forward

Neither rain nor snow nor sleet nor hail
Oh Prabhupada, I'm reading your books
Whether free, full price or even on sale
You open my eyes so I can envision a better look

Your passages help me to stay alive
Twenty-four hours, every second, every minute
"It Don't Come Easy" mind you, I work hard to strive
Your purports contain loving ingredients, necessary for me to survive

It makes no difference what anyone else thinks
They don't know what I'm really about
Sometimes Prabhupada I'm on edge, on the brink
Others times, I'm batting .406, in Krishna's groove, highly devout

When I'm on the road at a fork, stuck in the middle
I diddle and daddle and doodle playing life's fiddle
It's very difficult at times to make the right choice
Whatever road I choose Oh Prabhupada, I always hear Krishna's voice

Prabhupada Comes To America

He left Calcutta in sixty-five
Not a penny to his name
Thirty-seven days aboard a cargo ship
His health began to wane

Vomiting, dizziness, and heart attacks
Are what he had to endure
Left Boston Harbor for New York City
Krishna said, "Be rest assured"

After three weeks in Gotham Town
The city to him was home

He didn't know people at that time
But said, "I am never alone"

Visiting America was a big decision
Opportunities to express his spiritual master's vision
Spreading Krishna consciousness was the mission
He knew people in many cities would listen

Anywhere Krishna sends me, is home
He provides shelter wherever I roam
Temples all over the world, was his dream
He was a patient man, with high esteem
We have a long way to go, you know what I mean

Krishna is here to ensure our protection
Leap over life's obstacles under My grace and direction
"Got My Mind Set On You" is a great Harrison selection
Depend upon Me, I love you with no exceptions

Krishna's will sent Prabhupada to New York's Lower East Side
People in Manhattan were seeking a higher spiritual guide
Searching for something beyond life's ordinary ride
Like surfing the *Bhagavad-Gita* with Krishna at high tide

One must be pure inside and out
Chanting in purity brings spiritual clout
Desiring material pleasure you can live without
Be true to yourself, three strikes and you're out

Swamiji was the one who could show them the way
He guided us "Faster" on The Hare Krishna Highway
It was time for him to consider his medical condition
Upon returning from India, he continued his mission with superior intuition

Release what's old and accept the new
No more Swamiji, it's Prabhupada now to you
Let go of what doesn't work and remember Krishna is True Blue
The more you chant, Hare Krishna
The more Krishna loves you

Prabhupada Comes To London

George Harrison and The American Krishnas in London they did meet
They graced Lord Krishna standing at His lotus feet
George spoke of his spiritual quest and realizations of karma
The Krishnas greeted George as expressed in their dharma

George realized there was something more to everyday life
He felt at home with Krishna in spite of his daily strife
George could see the complete picture when the pieces of the puzzle fit together
He was certain Krishna would protect him in spite of stormy weather

Prabhupada was pleased to hear of the spiritual deeds George performed
People turned to Krishna because of the many hearts Harrison warmed
Serving Krishna through his music, George sang the Lord's name in his songs
A plainclothes devotee, George was a pied-piper who banged on Buddha's gong

Powerful and spiritually advanced Prabhupada was always humble
Harrison liked this trait in Bhaktivedanta who said stay with me, you will not stumble
George learned from a lot from Bhaktivedanta's example
Prabhupada showed the world what he wanted, and it normally was ample

George spent an eternity chanting Hare Krishna
He told the Lord I never wanna miss Ya
This always put George in a loving meditative trance
Let our relationship be a lifetime spiritual romance

Prabhupada The Genius

Prabhupada lived a simple life
He was never out of touch
Like President, John F. Kennedy
His followers adored him very much

Prabhupada possessed a reassuring look upon his face
A gentleman with style, stature, and plenty of grace
A similar stare as President, Theodore Roosevelt
Prabhupada was sophisticated, smart, and svelte

Neither men had concerns about taking a lick
Teddy said, speak softly and carry a big stick
When making a point, Prabhupada cut to the chase
The dictionary under ISKCON shows a photo of Prabhupada's face

A.C. Bhaktivedanta knew how work a crowd
Krishna devotees support made him very proud
The new book "Krsna" just hot off the press
Sold out in San Francisco in a few minutes or less

Prabhupada said in Nairobi, "Keep me talking – that is my life"
You can agreee or disagree, that's my decree
Don't let me stop talking, I'm ISKCON's Master MC
Nobody comes close, maybe Howard Cosell or Muhammad Ali

Prabhupada was a genius, visualizing many steps ahead
He knew opponents moves, staring them down with a feeling of dread
Outwitting adversaries, match play advantage in Krishna's favor instead
A.C. Bhaktivedanta could turn on a dime wishing then you were dead

As expected Krishna Consciousness spread to every village and town
There wasn't a place where Krishna couldn't be found
Available for everyone it was a definitive breakthrough
Lord Caitanya's prediction was certainly coming true

Krishna Consciousness is inside of everyone, let it flow and reveal
It's always within you, never hidden nor concealed
It simply has to be revived in order to be kept alive
Our inner core must be open and ready, to feel Lord Krishna's presence and survive

A.C. Bhaktivedanta chose his moments carefully
He knew when to hold 'em and when to fold 'em
When to throw the curveball and when to throw the fastball
A mindful leader with powers of steel, writings of Lord Krishna, absolutely ideal

The A. C. Rap

Krishna addiction
A loving affliction
Swami's conviction
Caitanya's prediction

"Gita's" the solution
The new constitution
ISKCON evolution
The Krishna revolution

You're never alone
In the Hare Krishna zone
Krishna consciousness roams
In A. C.'s home

It's everyone's dream
He's soul supreme
Complete's the scene
You know what I mean

Nothing is finer
Than a Harrison one liner
"My Sweet Lord"
We're all aboard

"He's So Fine"
Gonna make Krishna mine
Rain or sunshine
Krishna's so divine

A. C. is smiling
In the spiritual sky
Can't ya see his grin
Get Krishna high

I'll be with ya
Every step of the way
Put the pedal to the metal
On the Krishna Highway

Give Thanks

Give thanks for a wonderful life and your loved ones in it
Love them with all your might, every second every minute
Forever in your heart, feel their presence, never be apart
Open your love with trust In Thee and abundance unfurled
Maybe someday this place will become a better world

Life

Not just a Post cereal
Or a board game-material
You gotta be spiritual
It's our time spent on earth
Until we're ready for rebirth

For whatever you do
It's a daily review
You gotta be proud
Just sing it out loud
So the Lord can hear

You know He's with you
Shouts out your name – Hey Yoo-hoo
Live each and every day
On The Hare Krishna Pathway
'Cause the Lord is so dear

You know it don't matter
If you're thin or you're fatter
If you're one or a twin
Just open your heart
You will always get in

CHAPTER 5

Govinda's of Tucson & The Krishna Temple

(Introducing Krishna Cove)

Krishna Cove

Chapter 5 Photograph Credits

Photographs Were Taken at Govinda's of Tucson & The Krishna Temple & Are the Property of Steven Leonard Schwartz Unless Otherwise Noted

Krishna Cove

Welcome To Govinda's in Tucson

Welcome To Govinda's in Tucson
Our Krishna Mind is always turned on
Whether we're eating, grooming, or resting
At Govinda's aviary, we're Krishna investing

So really enjoy and get into the fifth chapter
There's so much here for you to capture
It's easy to realize the beauty of Krishna's stature
We live everyday in Krishna's rapture

A Krishna Day

RECEIVED HONORABLE MENTION IN 1ST ANNUAL BHAKTIWRITER'S WRITING CONTEST (POETRY DIVISION)

Krishna, be with me while I'm sleeping
Keep me Krishnatized when I'm awake
May George Harrison always be divinely smiling
Loving You, Krishna, is no mistake

Krishna, Your message gives me brand new hope
Prabhupad marconied the morse code to You
My eyes see You clearly, magnified through the lens of a telescope
Your love shines through the material hullabaloo

Krishna, You filter my life's impurities
Every time I reach out to You

Shelter me with Bhaktivedanta's securities
You make certain I'm not feeling blue

Krishna, I'm glad You didn't slip away
Through my fingers leaving me sad and grey
It doesn't always have to be this way
I want everyday of my life to be "A Krishna Day"

Krishna, I turned myself all the way around
When I heard the Hare Krishna Mantra Sound
The Bhagavad-Gita keeps me Krishna bound
Thanks to Prabhupad, I'm Krishna found

Krishna, George sings, "My Sweet Lord"
It's bershert, it was definitely meant to be
I don't care for awards, chanting is my daily reward
My only desire is for You to watch over me

Climbing through Your window at such a great height
The darkness transitions into a bright, white, light
My sadness changes to gladness, entering Your sight
I believe in You Krishna, everyday and every night

A Traveling Monk

I'm a traveling monk for many days of the year
Delivering Prabhupada's message with devotion and cheer
My reward is service to Krishna and seeing devotees smiles
Krishna's not authorized to give me frequent flier miles

Anytime, anyplace, anywhere – Krishna, I'm at Your service
Anything I can do for You, I'm humbled and never nervous
The sun shines bright and glows so right with a Vrindavan hue
My photograph says it all My Lord, my love for You is true

Ananta Deva's Song

Change your perspective it's your Krishna elective
Have a higher perception it's your Krishna exemption
Have a determined conviction it's your Krishna prescription
Let me rise to the occasion on our Krishna liaison

Be at peace with me and let me be free
Please release me and balance my energy
Krishna, embrace me do not erase me
"Simplicity—Authenticity—Synchronicity"

Give me bliss, Your soft voice is here to stay
You penetrate my soul each and every day
I'm rock solid with You Krishna, I'm grounded today
You revealed Your sky of blue when George sang "Blow Away"

Wherever I am Your blissful electricity electrifies me
The rising of Your tides flows my mind with fluidity
Bless me as I awake and stay with me during the day
May I always walk tall on the Hare Krishna Highway

Be With Me Always

I'm in no hurry Hari, I'm in no hurry Hari
No longer being followed by the maya safari
You're my sire, my squire, my ultimate desire
George just sang a verse to become Krishna higher

Singing with George in the chorus of his Krishna choir
I enjoy serving You, Krishna, I'll never retire
Krishna, "Be With Me Always"
In Tucson, Arizona or in Honolulu, Hawaii

Everything To Me

There's all kinds of love
Absorb it like a sponge
Grab it with a glove
Harness it from Krishna up above

Lock on to its molecules
Because Lord Krishna always rules
The Lord's got free radicals
Going to Vrindavan on sabbatical

Connect to My free electrons
Always keep Your Krishna hat on
Ensure George Harrison's tea is always steeping
Be certain his willow tree is never weeping
And his weekly appointment with Krishna he's keeping

Lord, touch my anatomy
On any day but Saturday
Your "Peace Train" stopped and reinvested
Cause on the seventh day You rested

Don't wanna be a public spectator
Keep me connected to Your generator
Jump start my Krishna battery
The way they taught at The Academy
It's very easy for me to see
Lord Krishna, You mean "Everything To Me"

He's Everybody's Lord

He came from Vrindavan with His heart on His sleeve
He's everybody's Lord, you know what I mean
Teaches me "The Gita" – and what the purports mean
Loves it when I chant to the Soul Supreme
Says He's the Lord everyone can afford
George wrote about him, He's "My Sweet Lord"

It's Krishna Time

I desire to connect with You all of the time
No operator assistance don't need a dime
Stay with me always there is no rent
From the spiritual sky Your love is heaven sent

I want to serve You every week
And pray at the base of Your lotus feet
Reading *The Bhagavad-Gita* is my Krishna drink
It quenches my spiritual thirst and energizes my mind to think

I want to please You every day
I adore You immensely stay with me and never go away
Our love's not for sale it will never be returned
A permanent purchase all receipts have been burned

I want to be with You every second
At Your service whenever You beckon
My caped crusader and spiritual hero
Without You Lord, my life would be worth zero

Krishna Nation

I just arrived in Tucson my Krishna hat is already turned on
Stepping off the plane my mind forgets the confused and insane
Walking slower and thinking only Krishna thoughts
Anticipating a smiling Prabhupad and Govinda's cooking a lots

I close my eyes, take a deep breath and slowly let it out
Knowing I will soon be chanting with Mataji Sandamini and her devotees devout
No one is keeping score who wins or loses, that's not what this is about
It's about seeing more sight through my eyes and absorbing more in my Krishna spout

A short one minute walk from my bungalow along the paved Krishna trail
Through the illuminated archway in the morning darkness I see Krishna's Holy Grail
I've arrived at The Temple, Rasa Raj is singing to all in his peacock wail
What colorful feathers has he, if we're lucky his plumage will prevail

Leila is a Tucson, Arizona survivor, with Krishna's blessing she was selected
To be the publisher of my three year spiritual journey, she was elected
When *Sweet Serenity* makes the New York Times best selling list
The Tucson Krishna Temple will have plenty of gratification and bliss

Krishna Real

Krishna, it's so hard to change
Turn everything around and rearrange
My mind's so crazy I'm almost deranged
Keep me from being returned or exchanged

Krishna, teach me to cope so my mind don't elope
"If Not For You" I wouldn't have range nor scope
If the bird named Phoenix can fly, that gives me hope
Rescue me Krishna I'm on my last rope

Krishna, I want to live within myself
Not a chameleon changing colors to save himself
I must get it together and repair my health
I've just retired so it's not the wealth

Krishna, encourage me to develop a regular routine
Not a scatterbrain life with anything obscene
I want to be a living and breathing Krishna machine
Got to keep experiencing Bhaktivedanta's dream

Krishna, register my number, get me back in the race
Start off slowly and keep a steady pace
Keep me keeping on not falling away from grace
Thinking of You keeps a smile upon my face

Krishna, keep my heart always open, I'm making an appeal
My love wants to show, it's ready to be revealed
I'm buckled in the driver's seat of Bhaktivedanta's Krishna mobile
George is riding shotgun and we're keeping it "Krishna Real"

Lalita

What a treasure, such a pleasure
No one could be sweeter
Ramesh and Ruky's daughter, Lalita
A little Rama Sita

Just two and a half years
More mature than her peers
Admired by Krishna and all of his seers
Touched my heart with emotional tears

The highlight of the morning chanting
Beautiful growth from a seedling's planting
Lalita's love of Krishna is enchanting
Already Krishnatized, doesn't require replanting

The twinkle sparkling in her eyes
Is sent with love from the spiritual skies
Pure and innocent there's no disguise
A lovely person for us to realize

My Krishna Best

Krishna shadows me as I walk
Krishna's in my speak when I talk
Krishna's in my sight when I see
Krishna loves me just because I'm me

Krishna's in my mind as I think
Krishna helps me swallow when I take a drink
Krishna's with me as I travel north, east, south, or west
Krishna's tests me so I'm always my Krishna best

Nothing To Fear

I worked all my adult life then it disappears
A couple bills then everything's in arrears
All of my smiles have turned into tears
As long as You love me, Krishna, there's nothing to fear

Prabhupada Consciousness Blues

In your presence I feel the essence of your guidance, trust, and, love
Your shining rays of light, entering my heart, reverberate from above
You lift me up to another level, when the rushing waves of the tide are high
Always be by my side whenever I call, and give me the strength to cope and
rise above it all

Prabhupada Humility Blues

I've never felt such humility
Bowing in your presence, so visibly
Insuring my survival in the material world with sanity
As everything around me becomes a calamity

Adoring you with a garland of flowers
Rose petals at your lotus feet
I felt the energy of your amazing powers
Humbled by your graciousness bestowed upon me

You open my eyes to see life's reality
Krishna gives me such a vitality
An irreplaceable feeling I did realize
The awe of that moment I can always visualize

Prabhupada May I Always

May I always feel the radiance emanating from your presence
Your eternal grace is such a beautiful present
May I always catch a glimpse of your shining inner light
Your guiding rays provide such a wonderful insight

May I always be in equilibrium and balanced when thinking of you
Your wise thoughts embrace me so I can easily say, Bhaktivedanta, Yes I Do
May I always perform a loving service and rise to the occasion
Your house that you built welcomes me for a lifetime liaison

May I always be at peace and material world released
Your voice empowers me to feel the jolt of your blissful electricity
May I always be open to hear a different point of view
Your footsteps remove me far away from the world's trojan horse, my guru

May I always be associated with devotees like The Tucson Crew
Your spiritual connection with Sandamini and The Little Boy Blue stand true
May I always have the strength to walk away from what's unwanted and untrue
Your devotee Gurudas still follows your example, but I didn't have to tell you

Pure Bliss

Nirantara Dasa Acbsp, always gives of himself
Receiving Krishna's love is his personal wealth
A humble man, he looks at life with the cards he's dealt
Like A.C. Prabhupad he watches his health

Nirantara Dasa Acbsp, was born to serve
The thread of his being is meditative and reserved
No one is like him he's Krishna worthy and deserves
He speaks Krishna's message from his heart, a lifelong yearn

The modern day spokesman for Bhaktivedanta
Any purport he translates into a George Harrison mantra
Singing lines of "Pure Bliss" from *The Bhagavad-Gita*
Filled with Krishna's love cause nobody does it sweeter

I call him The Voice, he's on Krishna's World Tour
Serving around the globe from Vrindavan to Mayapur
Be conscious of your Krishna consciousness is the message to endure
Chant with Nirantara Dasa Acbsp, be Krishna rich – that's the cure!

Pure Ecstasy

Krishna, Your spiritual tree is nothing but "Pure Ecstasy"
May my book, *Sweet Serenity*, serve You and be well received by the community
Please continue to be by my side and answer my prayers with sweet Krishna reality
May I continue to serve You, Lord Krishna, with the utmost love that can possibly be

Rasa Raj

My name is Rasa Raj
The Tucson Temple's glorious peacock
Keeper of the aviary entourage
Bill Haley said, that peacock really rocks the clock

My name has a Sanskrit derivation
A royal work of art is the translation
The pride of the peacock is the glory of God
I'm working for Krishna, just doing his job

I am the National Bird of India
I've got beauty, pride, and grace
A striking blue breast and neck
I'm fireworks all over the place

I've been painted, etched, and portrayed in cut glass
I show my plume with style and class
The most famous piece by Louis Comfort Tiffany
Whenever I see it, I have a Krishnatic epiphany

Sandamini's Place

My name is Sandamini, come chant with me
Our Temple is in Tucson, show your spirituality

We are the jewel of the cactus state
Enter through Bhagavad Gita's gate
"Walk This Way" don't hesitate
Don't be late for Krishna's date

Remove your shoes and stay a while
Chant the Lord's Name with class and style
Stay tuned to Krishna on the ISKCON dial
We love to see Bhaktivedanta smile

Sail with me on Sandamini's Krishna Cruise
Never be tangled up in attachment blues

With Krishna on your side, you will never lose
Bhaktivedanta says, "Lord Krishna Rules"

Be a Krishna Cowboy on Sandamini's Govinda Ranch
Maya attachments are no longer harassments
Krishna lassoed the last of the batch

Krishna is simply amazing
He's worthy of all our praising
Look at the lives He's saving
The sacred cows are grazing

I am "Rasa Raj," The Temple's glorious peacock
I rock the aviary clock
I've got beauty, pride, and grace
My magnificent plumage fireworks all over the place

"Shyam and Ram," we squawk "Krishna Talk"
It's like Bhaktivedanta and Gurudas taking a walk
It looks like we're fighting but it's all a Krishna show
You gotta give everyone their prasadam dessert you know

My palate screams hooray for Govinda's Cafe
I hope lasagna is on the menu today
I enjoyed my stay and will be back again someday
Krishna, be with me always on my spiritual highway

Shine The Light On Me

What an honor, a garland of flowers around you I did place
Completely overcome with joy as tears ran down my face
The feeling of that moment showing my devotion with emotion
My eyes shed so many droplets which could never fill your spiritual ocean

Prabhupada, I am totally moved in your Krishna groove
Feeling the pleasure from the imprint of a cow's hoove
Let me experience the bliss from Tucson, Arizona's Krishna's Cove
The special hideaway where Krishna's love freely flows

Shyam and Ram

We're Shyam and Ram, The Tucson Temple's prized macaws
We squawk so much, we act like in-laws
Shyam in Sanskrit means dark, black, and blue
Another translation is "The Name For Krishna, Too"

The Sanskrit meaning for Ram is pleasing
Shyam and me, we're always playing and teasing
The "Two of Us" together in our cage
We cause a commotion but always Krishna engaged

Put our names together we are pleasing Krishna
A really nice guy with a lot of charisma
We love serving Krishna it's our daily mission
Keeping Govinda's outside diners entertained
It's a Shyam and Ram Krishna tradition

The Gateway To Your Love

Walking through Your gateway from my Krishna bungalow
On the pathway to Your love it's everywhere I go
I'm chanting with The Tucson devotees, it's the only thing I want to do
My mind is focused, my heart is set, can't take my mind off of You

I solemnly open the Temple door, everyone is already there
Chanting Your Holy Name quietly, but with fervor and Krishna fanfare
One more tick it's five o'clock now, "Govinda" begins to play
I'm in my element with You Lord, and that's where I want to stay

The Tucson Temple Experience

No TV, no phone
Tell ET, don't call home
Tucson's Krishna Temple, "Sandamini's Place"
Made the pilgrimage there to see Krishna face to face

I'm here for a reason
Prabhupada and Krishna welcome me any season
Inhale and exhale I'm always Krishna breathing
The *Bhagavad-Gita*'s purports keep me believing

No one's pulling me in their direction
Don't need don't want I made a selection
Purify and simplify that's my election
Prabhupada and Krishna are my ultimate connection

Nityananda Das and his wisdom, a Stradivarius Violin
The mind controls the senses, intelligence controls the mind
Things that are negative have a purpose within, but
Too limiting an emotion aren't good for the Krishna inclined

Humbled by an honor bestowed upon me
Adorned Prabhupad with a flower garland, so graciously
Felt the energy flowing of his amazing powers
Bowing in his presence it seemed like hours

The Tucson devotees call me Bhakta Steve
Having the time of my life I didn't want to leave
I realized it later how relaxed I'd become
It's in my hands for Krishna to keep me His number one

Today and Everyday

The Lord gives us daily what we need to survive
A little more or a little less nourishment in order to stay alive
We evolve and revolve as one door opens another one closes
The Lord's love is so strong, He always proposes

We sikh out those who desire to live a life the spiritual way
Paving our future, brick by brick, along the way to Mandalay
I desire to live and play there "Today and Everyday"
And leave my body like George, chanting Hare Krishna and just "Walk Away"

Today's Big Deal

My Commander-in-Chief
I believe in Your beliefs
On any avenue or street
My feelings for You run deep

Lord, keep me posted within Your zip code zone
You provide me comfort when I'm on the road or at home
The world gives only a temporary fascination
Lord, You are my permanent stay-cation

Be with me always and never ever leave
My life without You I cannot conceive
I love to inhale Your glorious deeds
May I forever serve You with my heart on my sleeve

I wish there weren't daily temptations
Filling my mind with boggling situations
Causing repeated false impressions
Resulting in embarrassing confessions

Forcing me to jump through hoops
Taking detours and driving loop de loops
Are they placed there to see how fast I rebound
Are you watching if my feet stand upon the ground

To love You today much more than yesterday
The past is gone. You're now here to stay, hip hip hooray
May my action plan for tomorrow
Be approved by You and not be shallow nor hollow

Your love is permanent and very real
It's always exciting and filled with zeal
I will never trade it away for an apparent steal
Hey, Monty Hall, I already have "Today's Big Deal"

When I Get There

My shoes are worn and my body's tattered
Whatever I've been through, surviving left me Krishna battled
Don't want to wander aimlessly down an endless runway
Serving you Lord increases my humility "Day After Day"

"Any Road" You choose keeps my feet on the path You project
When I lay me down to rest I'm humbled that I'm one You protect
May I remain free and clear on a direct line to My Divine
Living my life with You until the "End Of The Line" is quite fine

I'm not blue anymore 'cause You won't leave me in my tears
Knowing I'm in Your thoughts eliminates my fears
No more galavanting "Here, There And Everywhere"
I know I'm home because Your love greets me "When I Get There"

KRISHNA COVE

A Krishna Singing Bird

Playing the harmonium while chanting Krishna's words
With such a lovely voice you are "A Krishna Singing Bird"
Vasanta Weiss, every Thursday your voice is heard
In India and around the world by every cowherd

So calm and collected, Vasanta, you are Lord Krishna selected
I've seen Him chant with you, you are Lord Krishna elected
At Krishna Cove's Kirtan your chanting is highly spirited
In India at the Ganges and in Egypt at the Pyramids

Krishna is Our Lord, He's stronger than any sword
Love Him on any accord, He's easy to afford
He's easily adored and is Our daily award
He's on George's guitar, on every note and in every chord

Yes, It's Lord Krishna, You make it all worthwhile
You take away our frowns and give us all smiles
You keep us spiritually high and maintain our Krishna lives
With a place like Krishna Cove, it's very easy to survive

Every Thursday Night

Hare Krishna Hare Krishna
We don't want to miss Ya
At The Krishna Cove every Thursday night
You improve our sight Krishna, by removing darkness from the night

The Krishna Cove offers a beautiful view
An atmosphere where any collegian can kirtan You
Rising so high in the spiritual sky
We may stay elevated forever, that's no lie

Your nectar's so pure
Never any artificial sweetener
Krishna is our spiritual cure
We're so happy to greet Ya

We chant to Your grace
As You fill our heart's space
You lift us higher and higher
Loving You is our only desire

For Aaron's Devotion

My devotee friend Aaron serves with loving devotion
With all his might not just a passing notion
Oh what a feeling an elevated elation
Irrational exuberance, a permanent Krishna stay-cation

Krishna will take you far if you think you can
He can sing the blues brother, he's Prabhupada's original soul man
He is Our rock and redeemer Our spiritual reservoir
Never gonna say to Krishna when in Paris, au revoir

Your free ticket is here to visit Krishna every Thursday night
Send everyone to Tucson, reach beyond your spiritual height
Go pass your spiritual past, climb onto Krishna's beanstalk tonight
Krishnasize your devotion, The Lord says it's all right

Turn off the oven, don't bake anything you're gonna loathe
No need to keep on wandering, don't need Miami's Coconut Grove
Take the Hare Krishna Highway and exit where you don't have to rove
You've reached your destination it's Tucson Arizona's Krishna Cove

The Hare Krishna Maha Mantra, just keep on chanting
You'll love it so much, keep on dancing and prancing
Nothing better in this life, Krishna Is the superb sensation
Absorb all the wealth, open the door to Krishna's manifestation

Millions of opulences are of no use to me
In times of trouble they do nothing to save thee
Krishna, may Your vision always be crystal clear in my mind
What a beautiful find to cope with life's daily grind

KRISHNA COVE

Krishna Cove

Krishna Cove is the place on Thursday nights you can just relax and chill
For an hour and a half, no hassle from a roommate, just be at will
Everyone from around town is coming by to chant a few rounds
It's very easy, man, to get into Krishna's Mantra sound

Our guitar will always be Hare Krishna smiling and shining
George Harrison is driving "Faster" in his sports car and will soon be arriving
Krishna, "I'm a Believer" and Bhaktivedanta is my "Dream Weaver"
"It Don't Come Easy" but hanging around campus doing nothing isn't much fun either

We've "Come Together" in Tucson to serve You better, "My Sweet Lord"
"Our House" is Founder Acharya certified to love You on any accord
"Here Comes The Sun," said George, may Krishna shine His bright, white light on you
The students are movin' to Krishna's groovin' and it's really Krishna soothing

Thank You Lord for inviting us to be with You
Everyone here feels Your love and knows You're True Blue
Because of You, our hearts will be more often Krishna divining
When George Harrison arrives for tea we'll serve him English Twining

Krishna Prema Suprema

Everyone is welcome, everyone is special
Spreading the word about Krishna Cove is essential
You're so bliss Oh Lord, The Krishna Cove is a reflection of You
The Krishna Cove welcomes You to Tucson, How Do You Do ?

The seeds from Your heart have been planted today
Don't need miracle grow, Your spiritual beanstalk is on its way
Everyone's voice at The Cove paves the way to Vrindavan
Because of You we're not Krishna starving, the price is really a bargain!

Krishna Prema Suprema
Our Lord, Our Sweet Spiritual Being
Open our eyes so we see what we should be seeing
Free us from the darkness that lately we've been feeling

Happy go lucky, Krishna, we are maya free
Within the walls of The Krishna Temple Library, we chant simultaneously
We're led by Vasanta Weiss or by anyone who says Krishna, it's my turn let's go
It's "Some Kind Of Wonderful" when everyone at Krishna Cove feels the chanting flow

My Sweet Nectar Flows

Show your love just chant and let it out
The Lord knows you're Krishna Cove devout
Obeisances to devotees who travel to Krishna "Roundabout"
In every village and town Prabhupada says you will find out

Let your fantasy be your ecstasy
Krishna's not concerned how your rubber burns
Show Him you're driving and you're racey
For every season, "Turn! Turn! Turn!"

Let your fashion be your passion
A full plate for Krishna, no prasadam ration
Krishna loves what's happening here
His Cove is filled with excitement and cheer

Krishna desires a full portion
To Krishna Cove and their good fortune
He smiles and screams "Hare Krishna"
Thanks Bhakta Aaron, every Thursday night kirtan
Will never miss ya, will always be there to bliss ya

Your good intention shows and always glows
Open the spigot so my sweet nectar flows
Sing to Thee with your utmost energy, so happily
From the rooftop of Apple they sang "Let It Be"

The Brand New Jewel

You're welcome to sit in some peace today
Krishna Cove in Tucson is the meditative way
It's only the beginning – it's only just the start
Chant Hare Krishna and open up your heart

The college spirit of the Arizona Wildcats is welcome here
"Come Together" with Krishna in a relaxed atmosphere
Attend Krishna Cove with your friends each and every week
Opportunities to meet someone new, have fun, and speak

It's a place where everyone knows your name
No one here cares about fortune or fame
Krishna Cove is the brand new jewel in the Arizona desert
It's our tasty dessert and Krishna makes it pleasant

Today is Thursday, it's not just "Another Day"
We are the ones who desire to "Walk This Way"
Walk Shiva's Walk and Talk Shakti's Talk
Don't mess with Krishna's elephant friend Ganesha
He's a University of Kansas Jayhawk

Thursday, Thursday

Oh what a feeling! It's real! I'm believing!
Krishna consciousness I'm achieving!

Chanting and singing the names of The Lord
At Tucson's Krishna Cove, everybody comes aboard

Come by and join us every Thursday night
Meet some new friends you will feel all right

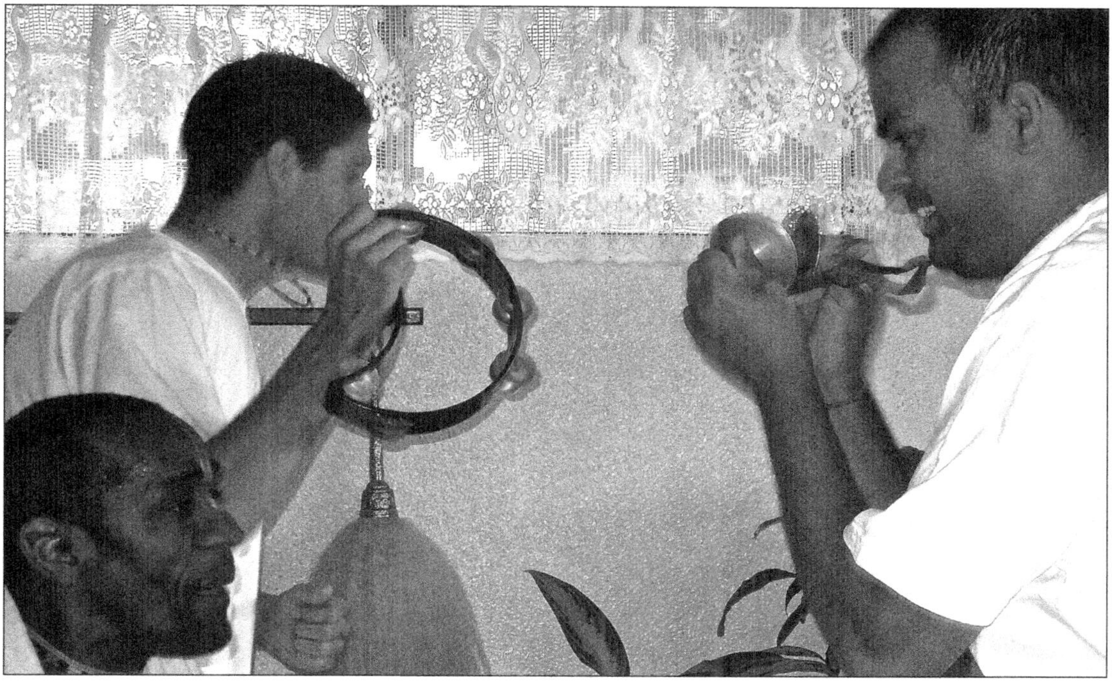

CHAPTER 6
ISKCON Temple in Honolulu & The Buddhist Temple in Maui

"A JOURNEY TO PRABHUPADA'S ROOM"

"FROM THE TEMPLE FLOOR" (photo tour)

"FROM THE TEMPLE GROUNDS" (photo tour)

"ON THE TEMPLE WALL" (photo tour)

"THANK YOU MADANA"

"THE BUDDHIST TEMPLE IN MAUI" (photo tour)

Chapter 6 Photograph Credits

Photographs Were Taken at the ISKCON Temple in Honolulu
& the Buddhist Temple in Maui
They Are the Property of Steven Leonard Schwartz
Unless Otherwise Noted

A JOURNEY TO PRABHUPADA'S ROOM

A Krishna High Five

Standing on ground zero Houston
I'm looking up to the spiritual sky
I know all you guys are rooting
For a smooth landing and "A Krishna High Five"

A journey of a lifetime begins with one step
Anticipating a good voyage, it will be worthwhile you bet
Holding the bannister advancing to the upper level
Krishna assures Prabhupada notices my revel

Past the open window up high on the wall
I make the turn around the corner
Krishna says keep on moving and stand up tall
No need to be scared like Little Jack Horner

I've touched down on the upper level
Visiting with the Founder Acharya will be very special
Lord Krishna's remarks I will never forget
I see him now, what an astonishing moment

Answer My Prayers

Krishna, tonight's the night You answer my prayers
I've got to make it all the way upstairs
I'll climb the tallest mountain to its highest peak
I need Your love now, don't want to play hide and seek

Krishna, I'll swim for miles in the deepest ocean
What a feeling to experience Your love and devotion
To see You standing on the shore at high tide
I'll surf the biggest wave till I feel You inside

Krishna, I don't want to ask for much
I desire to feel Your magical touch
I only need my daily fair share
My admiration for You is beyond compare

It's easy to love You when my heart is in gear
So happy to see You I won't shed a tear
In the afternoon sun I see Your face glistening
Whatever I say Krishna You're always listening

Planet Prabhupad

I've almost reached "Planet Prabhupad"
And the feeling surrounding me makes me glad
As a matter of fact it's like being on "Cloud 9"
I am in awe of the man in front of me and "I Feel Fine"

Aloha Krishna

I'm in Your island home
Where Bhaktivedanta roamed
During his stay in the seventies
I feel his amenities and material world remedies

Thank You for giving me peace and serenity
Your sweet nectar and love are so heavenly
I'll accept them in doses slowly and steady
So there's plenty to keep me happy and merry

Open Window

Fly through my open window with Krishna
There's plenty to learn I know so I'll teach you
Let Krishna invite you to my really big show
He's got your "Ticket To Ride" and away we go

Be Determined

(Prabhupad speaks to Bhakta Steven)

Be determined in life whatever you do
Your mother, Sylvia, said, "The will to do will carry you through"
Overcome the odds, Bhaktivedanta is living proof
My mission began with nothing under a leaking Manhattan roof

In a small New York City room with a burnt out light
I hunted and pecked on my Smith Corona day and night
Speaking of your mom and her point of view
Your mother, Bhakta Steven, was your first guru

She said, "Rest if you must but never quit"
Krishna is always with you I have to admit
The seed your parents planted have borne Krishna fruit
My *Bhagavad-Gita* principles have certainly taken root

The title of your book, *Sweet Serenity*, is a very nice amenity
Dedicating it to George Harrison will keep alive his musical heredity
It will open the eyes of devotees who are learning and yearning
Any Krishna conscious person should read it who's deserving

"Your I Will is more important than your IQ"
If Bhaktivedanta could do it so can you
Your photographs depict a lovely interest in ISKCON
It's proof my spiritual master's desire will never be gone

Your poetry is not ISKCON scripture but it certainly magnifies
How beautiful your writing is under "the spiritual skies"
I had you in mind, Bhakta Steven, when I said keep on writing
Your three year effort is inviting, the world knows it is enlightening

FROM THE TEMPLE FLOOR

FROM THE TEMPLE GROUNDS

A Promise to Myself

Be as tolerant as Honolulu's 51 Coelho Way's banyan tree
Plant your roots firmly in Krishna consciousness admirably
Remember to think of Prabhupada and Me universally
Very thankful to Madana Peat for her Krishna generosity

The Honolulu Ganesha Rap

My name's Ganesha you're a friend of mine
Come to me when your life's on the line
Don't ask the audience or phone a friend
Use my lifeline I'm here to defend

I block the obstacles in your way
Keep the traffic flowing on the spiritual highway
I give you hope to cope in the world today
Life shouldn't be crazy every day

My mouth is small so no gossip today
One tusk is gone I threw the bad one away

My head is big 'cause I'm thinking every minute
My tiny eyes are focused to their limit

My ears are large to hear your moans and groans
Don't gather no moss be a rolling stone
I do what I can so your heart don't bleed
Ganesha tries his best to make it all succeed

My tummy is large I can digest it all
Watchful of the good and the bad I'm always on call
Even though my belly's full, I never compromise
I love my prasadam it keeps me keeps alive

The Mouse keeps all our desires in check
Because we can't trust our own intellect
He saves us from the darkness of the night
George was right, keep looking for the light

My hands symbolize that you are blessed
Namaste, peace and love, please be at rest
Every day we're alive we gotta pass the test
There's no straight pathway to achieve success

I love all my friends in the USA
If there's too much worry just "Walk This Way"
If it ain't working you gotta find a better way
Because tomorrow is just "Another Day"

ON THE TEMPLE WALL

Krishna, There's No Other Love

Standing right in front of You
You see me as no one else can view
Providing rays of sunlight to a gratified, Prabhu
There's no other love anywhere, like You

You give me everything I need
Humble me and eliminate the greed
Bring me back home to the house You built
Always smelling like a rose, Your garden never wilts

You provide all the tools for me to succeed
Nurture my seedling with Krishnality and Godspeed
There's no other love anywhere, like You
George was right when he said, "I Live For You"

THANK YOU MADANA

Madana's Krishna Space

I just met Madana in her Krishna space
The Coelho Street Temple overflows with Prabhupad's grace
She welcomed me inside to tour the Temple place
And said Hari Bol! with a smile upon her face

THE BUDDHIST TEMPLE IN MAUI

The Maui Buddha

The Buddha spirit is inside of me as he visits early and often
He has me feeling sensational and directs my anger to soften
Buddha's face and go-lucky feeling exhilarate me to a higher altitude
I live a life with optimism as I reposition my longitude and latitude

Buddha is my buddy and accompanies me everywhere I go
I'm Buddha-licious from the top of my head to the tips of my Buddha toes
The Buddha travels with me no matter where I am
The United States, China, Switzerland, Bangkok, or even Vietnam

The Buddha keeps me mellow 'cause I'm that kind of fellow
Unlike Ganesha, Buddha don't leave footprints in my strawberry jello
He's played with Arthur Fiedler his instrument is the cello
The Buddha loves Donovan especially his "Mellow Yellow"

CHAPTER 7
Srila Prabhupada's Western World Headquarters Los Angeles, California

Chapter 7 Photograph Credits

Photographs Were Taken at Srila Prabhupada's Western World Headquarters in Los Angeles, California and at the 2011 Ratha Yatra in L.A. They Are the Property of Steven Leonard Schwartz Unless Otherwise Noted

RATHA YATRA 2011

PRABHUPADA'S GARDEN

Serving You with Love

It is a Friday morning in November, on Watseka Avenue in Los Angel-eez
Sitting on a bench in Prabhupada's private garden, there is very little breeze
Traveling through the pages of the *Bhagavad-Gita* gives me a spiritual identity
Serving his spiritual master was what he was after, with a "Sweet Serenity"

Named "My Sweet Lord" by our dear friend George Harrison
Krishna, "Serving You With Love" there is never any comparison
I see You in my viewfinder while photographing Bhaktivedanta's garden
In one hour Nirantara Dasa Acbsp will arrive to enjoy a hearty prasadam

Prabhupada's Garden

Just arrived on the Watseka Avenue Temple grounds
I can't believe all the peace I've found
Behind the Los Angeles Temple is a very special place
A beautiful garden, A.C. Bhaktivedanta's private meditation space

The banana trees gently rustle in the morning breeze
Everything is peaceful everything is at ease
I'm so relaxed, I wish every day would be like this
In Prabhupada's garden with Krishna, what a bliss!

The sky is crystal clear there is no haze
I just arrived at Prabhupada's Garden, but it seems like days
A "Krishnatic" feeling shadows me to and fro
Wanna keep it forever and bottle it, and never let it go

Sitting down on a wooden bench
Extending my arms out at full length
I close my eyes and my body's deflated
Totally relaxed, yeah, I finally made it

Reached such a level of inner peace
As if my life started over with a brand new lease
The feeling can be captured in another simple way
Keep the *Bhagavad-Gita* in your heart, every moment, every day

My facial expression says I'm in the right place
The lines on my face have disappeared from their space
A gentle grin captures A.C. Prabhupada from within
I could sit here forever softly playing Krishna's violin

Prabhupada
Society for Krishna Consciousness

My Krishna Life

Krishna, please release me from my struggle
Let me be free from the maya jungle
May Your spiritual energy deliver me to my destination
Krishna, open my mind so Your higher nature flows with no hesitation

Every day I'm on the line to direct connect with You
Don't need a seven or an eleven for my dreams to come true
I can see You Krishna in any frequency or bandwidth
I want to serve and love You transcendentally, forthwith

I chant so much I'm gonna have a spiritual revival
The power of my chanting is imperative for my survival
Fine tune my mind so I'm closer to You and not spiritually blind
Thank You again, Krishna, You're so so kind

May my intelligent soul keep me in the proper direction
Don't let me indulge and hurt my spiritual complexion
Keep my fish in the water swimming in Your direction
Keep my ship on course, steer my Krishna resurrection

NIRANTARA DASA Acbsp

Krishna's Hands

Leave it in Krishna's hands
Follow his commands
Doesn't make demands
His love only expands

Sweet Blue Boy
Krishna's the Real McCoy
He's 100 percent detached
Never seen anyone so relaxed

Open up Krishna's gate
Step inside don't hesitate
Don't wanna be late
It's a "Simple Twist of Fate"

Not loving Krishna is really absurd
Because Krishna is "Free as a Bird"
He's got Prabhupad's password
The clue is bird is the word

Welcomed in open arms
Enamored by his charms
Reading Prabhupad's purports and psalms
Krishna only calms

Krishna gives second chances
His love only enhances
He gives me admiring glances
My love for Krishna only advances

Don't need an ashram
Don't need a church
Krishna won't leave you in a lurch
Stand tall on Krishna's perch

INSIDE THE TEMPLE

RATHA YATRA

Mahatattva Das
Bhakta Terrence
Rajesh & Radhika
Jaya Keshava Das

Lord Krishna

That far east guy named Krishna
I love Him yes it's true

He keeps me on the straight and narrow
From a Gita point of view

The looking glass He sees me through
Reflects back on my life

To help me cope and give me hope
And deal with all the strife

Oh, Krishna Krishna Krishna
Where are You tonight

Open my eyes so I can realize
The darkness from the light

Oh, Krishna Krishna Krishna
Don't go too far away

I want You near 'cause You're so dear
You keep me on Prabhupad's way

The Sense Object Blues

My Lord, help me be firmly fixed in Krishna consciousness
I desire to rise above the world's material mess
With help and guidance I can pass your spiritual test
Elevate me to a level that's higher than the rest

Krishna, remind me to be like a turtle
Have my shell resemble an armored girdle
Let me overcome the sense object hurdle
May my soul within be strong, not weaken and curdle

Krishna, quiet my tongue so I won't be rude when I speak
Turn off my mind so my brain can't illicitly think
Deafen my ears so my hearing can't remember obnoxious language that wreaks
Close my eyes so my vision won't be tempted to sense object seek

Krishna, let me always experience a higher taste
I've come a long long way to reach the entrance to your spiritual gates
I'm a teenage mutant ninja turtle, ready to battle for the highest stakes
This is my final answer, Krishna, no more maya mistakes

CHAPTER 8
Special Spiritual Souls

Photographs are the property of Steven Leonard Schwartz unless otherwise noted

Chapter 8 Photograph Credits

Photographs Are the Property of Steven Leonard Schwartz Unless Otherwise Noted

Ode To Alice Cooper

It all began with a guy named Alice
Audiences were shocked with fright and malice
Chopping baby doll heads made his performance callous
The boa, the blood, the guillotine it's Alice right at us
Created theatrical horror with lyrics to harass
An Alice Cooper concert the original rock 'n' roll palace

Feeling summer in the city he composed "School's Out"
Released in seventy-two it packed tremendous clout
A mantra for kids everywhere Cooper's most famous single no doubt
Outraging parents, the social establishment, causing politicians to pout
"No More Mr. Nice Guy" wasn't about to give out

Alice welcomed to his nightmare the infamous Vincent Price
Whose ghoulish voice froze our soul into solid blocks of ice

The black widow infiltrated our mind weaving havoc her device
Ridding her from our brain required an antidote and a sacrifice

Tuxedo, walking stick, black top hat in hand
"Welcome To My Nightmare" was so very grand
Catapulted Alice to an upper band, he's now in high demand
No longer just a grain of sand, his music echoes through airwaves in every land

Washington, D.C. on high alert
Wasting our country becoming inert
Hear the wisdom from Mr. Alice Cooper
Take heed or remain in an oblivious stupor

Once elected selected and respected
No longer the choice you ain't got no voice
Open your eyes so you can realize
We got the power to execute your demise
You will be restricted and evicted it's no surprise

Hell has frozen over as The Hall of Fame ordered Alice to step right over
No need to grow that four-leaf clover
The mascara rock n roller from Detroit City
Earned the respect of the selection committee
Transformed his craft being witty and gritty
Reached the pinnacle of his career and he's still lookin' pretty

Alice in Cooperland

An Alice Cooper Tribute Band

Larry Cornwall

The Love in The Light in The Life

I am who I am, you are who you are
Collectively we are we, it's easy to see
Placed on this planet, there's a reason we are here
Someone's gotta man it, our home's in arrears

We've got to stay the course, 'cause we live for the cause
Feel the love at your heart's source, don't need no applause
You're part of the problem, if you're not part of the solution
Just Breathe Wellness Center is a Las Vegas Revolution

Don't be kept down with a monkey on your back
Be the divine leaf falling off the tree, release the slack
Photosynthesizing in the autumn, in the spring budding with glee
Fluttering in the cool October breeze, a hayride is fine with me

Meditate and feel great with Akasha and Aykanna
A little love and grace won't hurt you nor harm ya
Let the love in the light in your life say hello
Replace your karma with the glow from Sunny's halo

Song for George

(Tribute to George Harrison)
Ananda Vardhan 2010

Back in my teens
teenage dreams
nothing quite the same
you four lads
Liverpool
play it once again

like yesterday
you passed away
its been several years
your sweet songs never fade
drying up our tears

hardly knew you then
hardly know you now
nevertheless I must confess
I'd like to be your friend (repeat)

Radhe Shyam
Radhe Shyam
Radhe Radhe Shyam
Radhe Shyam
Radhe Shyam
Radhe Radhe Shyam

you make us sing
you make us dance
soon we'll be in trance
my sweet Lord
my sweet friend
nothing is by chance

hardly knew you then
hardly know you know
nevertheless I must confess
I'd like to be your friend (repeat)

Radhe Shyam
Radhe Shyam
Radhe Radhe Shyam
Radhe Shyam
Radhe Shyam
Radhe Radhe Shyam

Sri Radhe Radhe Radhe Shyam Govinda Radhe Sri Radhe
Sri Radhe Radhe Radhe Shyam Govinda Radhe Sri Radhe
Sri Radhe Radhe Radhe Shyam Govinda Radhe Sri Radhe
Sri Radhe Radhe Radhe Shyam Govinda Radhe Sri Radhe
Govinda Radhe Radhe Shyam Gopala Radhe Radhe Shyam
Govinda Radhe Radhe Shyam Gopala Radhe Radhe Shyam

(can be purchased on CD Baby)

Two Live HinJews

He's from Chicago his name is Gary Liss
At Krishna Lounge he humbled me into a state of total bliss
Traveled the world with his maven "Ain't Misbehavin"
I listened to his escapades with lifelong friend, Richard Slavin

Two Live Jews eventually became Two Live HinJews
A special pathway along "Any Road" they were paving
Didn't exactly know what they were looking for
Maybe a guru in Mandalay was their spiritual haven

The Lord promised you will find it and so much more
George said please look "Behind That Locked Door"
A five year journey together "Here, There, and Everywhere"
The cubbies split along "The Long and Winding Road" to find their separate fare

One to Israel and the other to India, desiring to be a sadu
To Nepal, The Himalayas, Cat Man Do, "Love Me Do"
Walking through the rice paddies of life, let your smile be your umbrella
Two Live HinJews at that very moment, said, "Do I know you fella?"

Mr. Gary Liss gives spiritual talks and is now Gary Prabhu
He takes healthy walks in the golden state on a beach called Malibu
Mr. Richard Slavin is a friend of us all as George Harrison introduced Bob Dylan
Radhanath Swami lives within the pages of *The Bhagavad-Gita*, with Lord Krishna he's always chillin'

Gaura Mani's Song

Sing from your heart
Chant loudly from the start
We will never be apart
My love for You, Krishna, is off the chart

Raise your hands up high
Reach for the spiritual sky
Chant His holy name and you'll get by
It won't take long 'cause you're Krishnafied

Hitch a ride with a devotee, they're all going His way
Six miles to Vrindavan on The Hare Krishna Highway
The Janmastami Festival is a special event today
Prabhupad built an air-conditioned tent where we can chant and pray

Be a part of Krishna's Birthday Show
Allow His sweet nectar to flow and overflow
Show Krishna how much you love Him so
Gaura Mani's gonna take us there, you know

You're just an ear's distance from Krishna's symphony
Wherever you are reach out for His spiritual electricity
There's never any cost or admission fee
Just chant out loud with Mataji Sandamini

The cows moo when Krishna moves and grooves
Chant His holy name and you will never lose
You will always be victorious because it's Krishna you choose
I'm with The Little Blue Boy, because Lord Krishna rules

Happy OM

HAPPY OM OH HAPPY OM
Ukulele me home
Your simple rhythm
Passes me through George Harrison's prism

Airy, Lively and Light
What a pleasant delight
Because of you tonight
I'm feeling pretty right

So wonderful tonight
HAPPY OM, just outta sight
It's all right – it's all right
It's all right – it's all right

Krishna Lounge, Las Vegas

Krishna Lounge, Las Vegas

Krishna Lounge, Las Vegas

Krishna Lounge, Las Vegas

Lilly & Friends

Sin City KISS
(A KISS Tribute Band)
Luis Reyes & Steve Mitchell are Las Vegas
(Gene Simmons & ChippenPaul Stanley)

The Backstage Bar & Billiards Blues

My name is Scot Coogan and I'm never losing
The Lord gets his fix while I'm banging my sticks
He loves my devotion as I'm moving to His grooving
No need to travel on Route 66 to get your drum solo kicks

I'm Ace Frehley's percussion man on the Space Invader tour
Ace don't need no gimmick, theatrics nor a lure
His electric juice is supplied by Thomas Alva Edison
Without a hitch Ace turns on the switch and creates rock n' roll medicine

I know the Lord is with me 'cause Ace told me so
That feeling flows freely through Frehley as "Shock Me" steals the show
The Lord blesses and blisses me, I see His vision in Traci's smile
Living large on the Vegas entertainment runway, her "Vogue" look is her everyday style

"Gimme a Feelin" I'm rocking and reeling drumming for Ace, this holiday season
It's a gift that's heaven sent, there's no rhyme nor reason says Jackie Gleason
Ace snared my life in this galaxy wanting the best he could see in the celestial show
The spaceman said how sweet it is, Scot Coogan, let's rehearse and away we go!

Sharing with Sharon

I'm sharing with Sharon to help the cause
The band's so meditative I can't stop my applause
The crystal ball has me vibrating up and down the walls
I'm talking to the Lord every time he calls

Let's meditate and pray and chant all day
If everyone donates the homeless situation might go away
Om is home for all of the homeless tonight
If we chant loud enough they'll have a place for the night

It's time we start thinking about others less fortunate
They're just like you and me, but we have a sleeping hut
Because what we have could all someday disappear
Losing a job or getting sick, we are the one whose hope is now fear

Gobinda in the Winter

Droplets of water drip from the spout
Continue to fall until they all spill out
One at a time flowing towards the drain
Won't stop dripping until you shut the main

Each snowflake is different with its own configuration
Everyone is special with a unique North Pole registration
It's scientifically determined they're never the same
"Gobinda in the Winter" it's an icicle flame

Send a chariot of horses all dressed in bows
Take me to wherever only the driver knows
My heart warms in the frigid cold
My love unfolds when my story is told

I'll drink a fifth, if Beethoven can bring it over
The Saint Bernard also covered for a box of Russell Stover
The chocolates shouldn't melt in the igloo's icebox
If it's not too much trouble, I'll take a bagel with cream cheese and lox

Just Smile

Just smile all the way through
The tunnel and the darkness surrounding you
Accelerate your mind on the destination you want to view
Just Breathe Wellness Center is the place you're going to

Go past your limit
No police chasing after you
In a few weeks you'll experience Simrit
And then we'll all get into it

The Lord's Surround Sound

When things are smooth and I'm in a groove
It's easy to see Lord, oh how You soothe
May I remember You always, my heart's source
Flowing freely within, Your servant, Steven Leonard Schwartz

When there's a calamity protect me from my insanity
Lord, please keep me humble, not lost within my vanity
Keep me believing, breathing and weaving through Your open window
Immersed within Your surround sound, outside, inside, above and below

Titiksava Karunika Dasa

Music Machine

My name is Wah!
I'm a Music Machine
"Love Holding Love"
You know what I mean

Thanks for showing up
You're gonna be heard
Sing along with me
You know the words

"Om Namah Shivaya"
I wanna take you higher
Stand up and dance
That's my desire

Take a "Leap of Faith"
That's all you gotta do
Krishna's in the house
Chanting next to you

"Open" up your heart
Be true to yourself
You get what I'm saying
Take your love off the shelf

You gotta job to do
Every day of your life
Love the one you love
Make a sacrifice

Show some action
Get satisfaction
It won't take long
Keep singing my song

By George, How Could I Miss

Ganesha, remove those obstacles from our lives
Make my soul smile I don't wanna despise
Start speaking the truth no more alibis
I'm in kirtan with Wynne all I see is Amma's eyes

Here comes Shakti my divine energy
My power source she electrifies you see
Animates the universe just magnify me
I'm all juiced up with Shakti electricity

Now I've entered the Shiva community
He provides my form and embodies everything
My ultimate light bulb it's an Edison thing
I'm shining bright 'cause my Shiva filament sings

All right Ganesha it's time to hit the switch
No power surge, it went off without a glitch
Dancing Shiva and Shakti just gave me the pitch
Let's get turned on, "By George" how could I miss

CHAPTER 9

Sat Nam Fest at Joshua Tree, California

featuring

GuruGanesha Singh

Chapter 9 Photograph Credits

Photographs Are the Property of Steven Leonard Schwartz Unless Otherwise Noted

A Bird Dressed in White

The innermost chamber within my heart
Stores the love that's been locked from the start
"A Bird Dressed in White" can unlock the passion
Her crystal clear voice is always in fashion

Open up your heart be true to yourself
That special someone waits to be herself
I know she desires more to be with me
"Dayndaa Day" holds the key to our destiny

May our love flow to each other, Wahe Guru
Milk and honey so sweet, a gift from me to you
The bird flies by singing "Hariaa" so magically
Embracing our love, living life so happily

The tide's rolling out as I skim stones in the ocean
See the ripples appear while standing on the beach
Our love's still here, it's just within an olive's branch reach
Just call me, Snatam, says the bird, smiling with devotion

A Place Called Joshua Tree

Let the person go
Who you used to be
Come out of hibernation
And fly with me

Flap your wings
To Joshua Tree
Sat Nam Fest
Is where I want to be

Unwind and let go
Exfoliate and glow
Let your spirit voyage flow
Let your hair hang low

I've gotta be me
Let the whole world know
A Yogi Bhajan Symphony
Let's get on with the show

It's time to begin
Take everything in
I'm ready to dream
Experience the scene

GuruGanesha and Paloma Devi
They're always ready
Rock the Lord steady
Size C Eveready

Dreaming of Sat Nam Fest

I don't have to wonder
What cloud I'm sleeping under
All roads converge on Joshua Tree
My time here will be simply heavenly

Now I'm a real somebody
Not an unknown geometric factor
My love is true with my favorite guru
GuruGanesha is here, "Love Me Do"

So far it's been nothing but the purest of bliss
The sun rises every morning around the bend at six
Let's "Walk with the Lord" the conductor shouts out all aboard
Everyone on the GuruGanesha train is singing, "My Sweet Lord"

The bird in white is my shining star
The rhythm of her voice echoes the Lord's spirit near and far
The most calm spirited person I've met in the world by far
A friend of us all, she's Snatam Kaur

GuruGanesha, you make the sun sing
"If Not For You" I wouldn't have anything
Your pure existence makes freedom ring
My dear old friend he's GuruGanesha Singh

GuruGanesha

Lovely melodies emanate from his riffs and chords
He shares with the world his craft, something he adores
His music effervesces when his guitar strings Singh
Ganesha is electric, eclectic and I select it, he's my everything

He's Yogi Bhajan's pied piper, singing words of peace
Ganesha is footloose and fancy free, like flying flocks of Canadian geese
His spiritual voyage has no boundaries, it crosses all meridian lines
The Guru's message is total bliss, he can't miss, it's so divine

Go with the flow, it's easy to let go
Hear his guitar echo during a Wahe Guru solo
Purify and simplify, he creates a different attitude
Elevate your spirit to a higher level, longitude and latitude

Mother MA-rgaret Gabriel comes to me
Her lifelong prayer answered, as my happiness comes to be
No one is more memorable in my mind than she
I close my eyes and she's here, right beside me

GuruGanesha Singh's

Let me tell you about a special friend
His name is Brother Steve
He loves the Lord to the very end
His poetry relaxes better than Alleve

He's compiling chapters for a poetry book
Each poem is better than the next
My music inspires him just take a look
"In the Light of My Soul" is always close to his vest

My Brother Steve is an expert in rhyming
He captures his readers with "Sweet Serenity"
His Nikon rings with photos of GuruGanesha Singh
Freezing me in the moment with precision timing

My lead singer from Miami is Paloma Devi
So outstanding is Paloma, she's my reality
Her voice is more powerful than a medieval dueling sword
George smiles when she sings her rendition of "My Sweet Lord"

Mooving to the Grooving

Get ready for a spiritual mission
It's not rocket science or nuclear fission
Just turn on the Lord's ignition
His spirit flows in all weather conditions
And emanates through the vents in the air condition

Open your heart, that's all you gotta do
Feel the love from above rushing through you
Sing "Walk with the Lord" in your Honda Accord or Subaru
"Mooving To The Grooving" on cruise control
Stay in the express lane, the Lord will pay the toll

Of Thee I Singh

I can feel it every moment I think of You
As the sun rises and sets Your love is true
Here it comes, says George, enjoy the view
Feel the warmth of its rays, sing Wahe Guru

You give the world peace and love from within your soul
Anyone hearing Your voice is now eternally whole
So many of us breathe freely this autumn season
We're living and believing, GuruGanesha, "you" are the reason

You light the world's flame and keep it flickering
Even though every day there's hatred and bickering
Sat Nam my brother, your love is a special I do
"Of Thee I Singh" is a tribute to my Boston Guru

"Walk with the Lord" and never turn back
May there be no darkness in our mind and no attack from Iraq
Let's go to the "End of the Line" there will be no police-ing
How sweet it is, said the great one, Jackie Gleason

Yogi Bhajan loves your enthusiasm and positive reaction
His litmus test gives a gratifying satisfaction
The magnificent aura surrounding you will never be broken
You are the Lord's gift to the world, the almighty has spoken

Bring us back to the Lord on his spiritual race course
You provide love in the light in the life direct from the source
"A Thousand Suns" is a shining bright star, of course
My poetry book is called "Sweet Serenity"
And my name is Steven Leonard Schwartz

Prayin' My Prayers

People I see and places I go
The Lord's with me now 'cause He told me so
He's my true religion I obey with ease
My lucky brand, with the SF Giants you gotta believe

I'm singing with Singh gonna "Walk with the Lord"
I'm standing tall on my own accord
The Lord's by my side keeps my spirit bright
I'm smiling with pride got me feeling just right

I'm "Prayin' My Prayers" with the guru man
GuruGanesha Singh, it's the Lord's command
The cat left the cradle for Yogi Bhajan
Not spinning his dreidel, he's a koala man

Proper Bostonian

There's something really special about you
The way you do the things you do
Painting a picture of the world with a universal hue
It's gotta have the GGS stamp of approval

You always give me the right time of day
As others are fleeting and go on their way
To and fro with silence and nothing to say
You keep me informed on the guru's highway

You're just that kind of a guy
It's easy for you to laugh and say hi
The Gods smiled upon you when they passed by
Let's raise him up to the highest level of the high

Because of you my spiritual flame shines bright
You remember my name in darkness or in light
Would save me a seat on the last flight out, that's right
You're GuruGanesha and I say that's all right

Sat Nam Fest

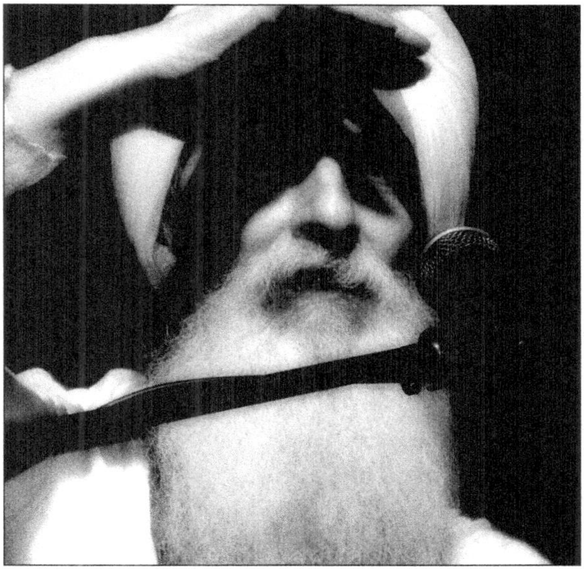

We've come today from near and far
By bus and plane, by taxi and car
Guided by the light of Yogi Bhajan's
shining star
I have my festivities ticket and halavah
from the bazaar

We've gathered at the sacred Joshua
Tree Park
For Sat Nam Fest from the Spirit
Voyage Ark
We're gonna rock before sunrise and
roll after dark
Forget about life back home and doing
shots of Cutty Sark

A jam-packed agenda is on for the four-day slate
I'm getting up early and going to bed really late
Here to recuperate, rejuvenate, meditate, and just feel great
Gonna romance with the Lord, couldn't have a better date

The mellifluous voice of Snatam Kaur
The bird in white I can listen for hours
She told me don't need, don't want, just be yourself
Fulfill your destiny, take your love off the shelf

GuruGanesha, that grin and Cheshire cat smile
Give me his music for miles and miles and miles
He's from my hometown, said to purify and simplify
The sounds from his guitar always get me high

The Ganesha Rap

My name's GuruGanesha Singh
Sat Nam Fest is happening
It's a beautiful thing
Let our music ring

Whatever it takes
Open your spiritual gates
C'mon don't be late
'Cause the Lord won't wait

We're here on a mission
Open your soul and listen
You will shine and glisten
No more toxic emissions

Let your love shine through
The haze, the clouds and the sun's hue
Create a much better view
The world wants a more beautiful you

Your spiritual insight
Is expanding tonight
Breathe freely and release what's uptight
"Don't Think Twice It's All Right"

The GuruGanesha Band

They play a funky spirit
So everyone can hear it
Singing praises to the Lord
The God we all can afford

The rhythm and the beat
Has everybody on their feet
No one's sitting in their seat
We're dancing to the Elite

Ganesha's the leader of the pack
Keeps everyone coming back
Playing music for you and me
He's a magician at harmonizing

GuruGanesha is jiving as he's smiling
With a new day dawning and the sun's rays rising
The Lord in our heart is arriving and thriving
I'm climbing the mountain, accelerating as I'm driving

That Ganesha guy just don't give it a rest
I see why Steve loves him—he's so spiritually blessed
He never holds back, always gives his best
He's playing for a Higher Authority, it's the ultimate test

The Guru's Smile

The Guru's smile stretches for miles
Through demarcation lines across zones of time
His Cheshire grin welcomes me in
To enjoy the beauty within and join the divine

The Guru's face is always mellow with grace
Spreading peace and love to the human race
He exudes warmth and calm to every possible place
I have a spaceship no longer am I "Lost in Space"

The Guru's eyes are experienced and wise
They've visualized a lifetime of truths and alibis
Focused through the lens photographed in his mind
Every frame's frozen, a scrapbook of all mankind

The GuruGanesha Band in concert, I'm rocking and reeling
Performing my favorite songs, they keep me believing
Ganesha's going strong, his spiritual voyage flame's still burnin'
Keeping the dream alive, it's gotta be that mystical, magical turban

The Voice

The new kid on the block
Solid as a rock, rock solid is she
The heart and soul of GuruGanesha's band
No introduction needed, she's Paloma Devi

Her sparkling voice leaves me no choice
An engine tender yet powerful, it purrs like a Rolls Royce
Reaches the high and low octaves, all over the scale
They come to hear her sing from Stanford to Yale

A little traveling music Mr. Maestro and away we go
Leaving Miami Beach for the really big show
Gonna be a "Bright Star" she's got the spirituality
She sings like Whitney Houston, with passion and vitality

This Joshua Tree

This Joshua Tree is a special friend to me
It's position is my guiding light
Breakfast and concerts exit my bungalow to the left
Sunrise at six and cover to this book, are a minute walk to the right

Today's George Harrison

The expression on his face cries for the human race
The look in his eyes wears no disguise as he pleads his case
His sincerity is eveready, his loving words to the Lord are very clear
To GuruGanesha, George Harrison is so very dear

Emotions similar to George, he realizes the world is coming unhinged
Small fires start slowly and then out of control the conflagration begins
Ganesha Singh brings peace and love to us all with his spiritual music
Feeling everyone's pain, he sings "A Thousand Suns" in electric or acoustic

Loving George for many years, in the photo he's ready to shed a tear
On a spiritual journey his bright star illuminates our lives for many a year
His band plays a mean version of George Harrison's "My Sweet Lord"
Lead Singer, Paloma Devi, sends me freewheeling with her beautiful chords

EPILOGUE TO GEORGE HARRISON (I)

Mother Nature's Sun

Well, I'm off into the garden to have some green fun
Hey, it's rising in the east, "Here Comes the Sun"
Look who I found nesting in old Acorn Tree
A roadrunner and her baby, call him "Mother Nature's Sun"

EPILOGUE TO GEORGE HARRISON (2)

Not Just a Wim

You are "My Everything" George "No Matter What" I do or where I go
"What Is Life" without your music and lyrics, I really wouldn't know
Thanks for being there whenever I call on "You" wherever I may roam
Forever a permanent fixture, not just a "Wim" I get advice from "the gnomes"

AFTERWORD

George found out early
From Gurudas how worthy
It is to have Krishna on his mind
This pleased Prabhupada and all of mankind

The *Bhagavad-Gita* keeps on flowing
Its purports are forever knowing
Eternally glowing is your soul
By His Example George became whole

CPSIA information can be obtained
at www.ICGtesting.com
Printed in the USA
FSOW04n0953210116
15973FS

9 781935 437918